Catherine Coucom

Cambridge IGCSE® and O Level

Accounting

Workbook

Second edition

CAMBRIDGE
UNIVERSITY PRESS

University Printing House, Cambridge CB2 8BS, United Kingdom

One Liberty Plaza, 20th Floor, New York, NY 10006, USA

477 Williamstown Road, Port Melbourne, VIC 3207, Australia

314-321, 3rd Floor, Plot 3, Splendor Forum, Jasola District Centre, New Delhi - 110025, India

103 Penang Road, #05-06/07, Visioncrest Commercial, Singapore 238467

Cambridge University Press is part of the University of Cambridge.

It furthers the University's mission by disseminating knowledge in the pursuit of education, learning and research at the highest international levels of excellence.

Information on this title: education.cambridge.org/9781316505052

First published 2018

20 19 18 17 16 15 14 13 12 11

Printed in Malaysia by Vivar Printing

A catalogue record for this publication is available from the British Library

ISBN 978-1-316-50505-2 Paperback

Additional resources for this publication at cambridge.org/9781316505052

How to use this book

This Workbook complements the IGCSE and O Level Accounting Coursebook and aims to help you consolidate your accounting knowledge and understanding and develop the skills of analysis and evaluation.

The Workbook has been designed as a flexible resource to support you on your accounting skills journey. The questions are designed to provide further opportunities for you to check your ability to provide solutions to a variety of accounting problems and practise your accounting skills.

Example 3.2

At the end of her financial year on 31 May 20–9, the totals of Rita's trial balance failed to balance. The total of the debit side was $98 730 and the total of the credit side was $99 176. She entered the difference in a suspense account and prepared a draft income statement. The profit for the year was calculated at $9 366.

The following errors were then discovered:

1   An invoice for goods sold on credit to Waqas had been entered in the sales journal as $1 100 instead of $110.

2   The purchases returns journal had been overcast by $100.

3   A new motor vehicle was purchased on 30 May 20–9. The total cost, $12 650, which included $340 for fuel and insurance, had been debited to the motor vehicles account. No depreciation is required for the motor vehicle for the year ended 31 May 20–9.

4   The total of the discount received column in the cash book, $82, had been debited to the discount allowed account in the ledger.

5   The balance of the petty cash book, $50, had been omitted from the trial balance.

6   Brian is both a supplier and a customer. Sales, $230, on credit to Brian had been credited to the account of Brian in the purchases ledger.

   a   Prepare journal entries to correct errors 1–6 above. Narratives are not required.

   b   Write up the suspense account showing all the necessary corrections. Start with the balance arising from the difference on the trial balance.

   c   Prepare a statement to show the corrected profit for the year ended 31 May 20–9.

Example – Examples of common accounting problems are shown.

The stages in producing the answer – Step-by-step guidance shows you how to solve accounting problems.

The stages in producing the answer

1   Go through the trial balance and the accompanying notes and label all the items.

   Put a label 'IS' against anything which will be used in the income statement.

   Put a label 'FP' against anything which will be used in the statement of financial position.

   Remember that anything in the trial balance is used once in a set of financial statements and any notes to a trial balance are used twice.

Tip – Tips set the context of the skills needed to provide the solution.

TIP
This question requires the skill of knowledge and understanding. You need to know the principles of double entry and you need to understand how to apply that knowledge to various business transactions.

Tips on improving this answer

1   In part **i**: mention should be made of the time period covered by the statement and the purpose of preparing it.

2   In part **ii**: a statement of financial position does not cover a period of time. Mention should be made of exactly what this document shows.

3   In part **iii**: capital can be introduced at any point in the life of a business. The explanation should indicate who introduced this capital.

Tips on improving this answer – Suggestions for improving an example solution show how even better answers can be provided.

A student produced the following answer... – Sample answers show how solutions to accounting problems might be approached.

Exercise

See if you can prepare improved answers to the theory questions.

When you have completed your answers, you can compare them with the suggested answers shown at the end of the section.

Exercise – Exercises invite you to provide your own solutions to accounting problems.

b i An income statement shows the income and expenses.

ii A statement of financial position shows the financial position of the business for the period.

iii Capital is the amount invested in the business at the start.

Partnership

Extract from statement of financial positon at ....

	$ Partner A	$ Partner B	$ Total
Capital accounts	XXXX	XXXX	XXXX
* Current accounts	XXXX	XXXX	XXXX
	XXXX	XXXX	XXXX

Templates – Templates show examples of the main types of financial statements for different types of trading and non-trading organisations.

4 On 1 June Bekele purchased goods on credit from Phayo. On 8 June some of these goods were returned. How did Phayo record the transactions of 8 June?

	Account debited	Account credited
A	Bekele	purchases returns
B	Bekele	sales returns
C	purchases returns	Bekele
D	sales returns	Bekele

Multiple choice questions – You have the opportunity to test your knowledge, practise calculations and analyse information through a range of multiple choice questions.

24 Waqas is a trader selling on credit terms. His financial year ends on 31 August. During the year ended 31 August 20–2, some debts were irrecoverable. At the end of the financial year, he decided to create a provision for doubtful debts.

a Explain the meaning of the following terms:

i irrecoverable debts

ii debts written off recovered

iii provision for doubtful debts

Waqas decided that the provision created on 31 August 20–2 should be 3% of the trade receivables and that it should be maintained at the same percentage of trade receivables at the end of each financial year. He provided the following information:

	$
31 August 20–2 Total trade receivables	5 500
31 August 20–3 Total trade receivables	6 200
31 August 20–4 Total trade receivables	4 900

b Write up the provision for doubtful debts account as it would appear in the ledger of Waqas for the three years ended 31 August 20–2, 31 August 20–3 and 31 August 20–4.

c Prepare a relevant extract from the statement of financial position of Waqas at 31 August 20–2, 31 August 20–3 and 31 August 20–4.

Structured questions – These give you the opportunity to practise solving a variety of structured accounting problems.

Introduction

This Workbook is designed to help you develop your understanding of accounting, to build up your skills and to enable you to assess your progress.

The book can be used in conjunction with the Cambridge IGCSE and O Level Accounting Coursebook, but it may also be used independently. Answers to all questions in this Workbook are provided on the accompanying Teacher's Resource.

Part 1 of the book explores what skills you need as an accountant, and how you can develop these. It also contains some sample questions with examples from the author of the stages you could go through when approaching these questions. It then guides you through the presentation of financial statements and why they are presented in a particular way.

Part 2 contains multiple choice and structured questions that are directly linked to the topics covered in the Coursebook. You can tackle a section of the book when you have completed that section of the Coursebook or you can choose to work through all the sections towards the end of your course. All multiple choice and structured questions, along with their answers, have been written by the author.

As with the Coursebook, this book seeks to cover all the topics in the syllabus and to provide you with the skills you need in accounting, and to strengthen your understanding along the way.

Part 1: Developing skills
Skills you need to demonstrate in accounting

This section of the Workbook looks at the range of skills needed by an accountant; these support the Cambridge Assessment International Education Accounting syllabus for IGCSE and O Level. It considers what the skills are, what they mean and how you need to be able to recognise their importance so as to improve your understanding of accounting.

1.1 Skills in accounting

There are three main skills needed in accounting:

- Knowledge and understanding
- Analysis
- Evaluation

We will consider each of these skills separately.

1.2 Knowledge and understanding

You should be able to:

- demonstrate knowledge and understanding of facts, terms, principles, procedures and techniques
- demonstrate understanding of knowledge through numeracy, literacy, presentation and interpretation and apply this knowledge and understanding in various accounting situations and problems.

The starting point when studying accounting is to acquire knowledge. This is the first criteria. Knowledge will be acquired as you study each section of the Coursebook. This involves learning about the key terms used in accounting and the processes for recording financial information. It is important to learn and be able to define the key terms in the subject and to understand what they mean.

Once that knowledge has been acquired, an understanding of the relevance of that knowledge will gradually develop. You will be able to use that knowledge to record day-to-day financial transactions and also to prepare financial statements.

The more you study the subject, the greater your knowledge about the subject and the more you will understand. The skills of knowledge and understanding take time. You need to learn the terms and processes and then develop an understanding of why these processes are carried out. Do not expect this learning process to happen overnight; your ability to know and understand will develop gradually. There is no substitute for practice in recording financial transactions and preparing financial statements. This is the best way to learn and understand. Knowledge and understanding together form the platform on which everything in accounting is based.

How to recognise when knowledge and understanding are required

Look out for command words. These should help you to recognise what you need to do.

Command words requiring knowledge and understanding include:

> balance, calculate, complete, define, describe, explain, give, identify, indicate, name, outline, prepare, state, suggest and summarise.

The following summarised question shows you how these command words can be used.

Example 1.1

A question provides a partially completed appropriation account and details about the balances on the books at the year-end and details of the partners' accounts.

The requirements of the question are:

Define the term partnership.

State one advantage of being a partner rather than a sole trader.

List two disadvantages of being a partner rather than a sole trader.

Suggest two reasons why a partner may lend money to the business instead of investing more capital.

Calculate the rate of interest which was charged on drawings.

Complete the appropriation account of the partnership.

Prepare the partners' current accounts.

Balance the accounts and bring down the balances.

Prepare the statement of financial position of the partnership.

Explain why the bank manager may be interested in the partnership financial statements.

Name two other business people who may be interested in the financial statements of the partnership.

Each part of this question requires knowledge and understanding.

TIP

The skill of knowledge and understanding includes definitions, basic principles, double entry, books of prime entry, bank reconciliation, financial statements (including year-end adjustments) and simple calculations.

How to demonstrate knowledge and understanding

To demonstrate your knowledge and understanding, make sure you read the question carefully. If you are required to explain or define terms, think about how you are going to express yourself. Plan what you are going to write and make sure you are not just repeating the information given without attempting to obey the command word. If you are required to prepare accounts, journal entries or financial statements, the requirement will be quite clear about what you have to do. Again, think carefully before you start writing. Use your knowledge and understanding of the topic and apply this to the scenario given.

1.3 Analysis

You should be able to:

- select data which is relevant to identified needs of business

- order, analyse and present information in an appropriate accounting form.

It is essential to have a thorough knowledge and understanding of basic accounting before attempting to apply the skill of analysis. As you develop your knowledge and understanding of the subject, so you become able to take the next step. This involves being able to analyse accounting information and draw reasoned conclusions. This skill requires practice. It cannot be learned by rote. Each scenario is different so you must be able to apply your knowledge and understanding to a given scenario and analyse the financial data provided.

How to recognise when analysis is required

Command words requiring analysis include:

analyse, calculate, comment, describe, explain, identify, select, state, suggest and summarise.

The following summarised question shows you how these command words can be used.

Example 1.2

A question provides a financial statement and other supporting information about the business of a sole trader, including details of errors made in the books.

The requirements of the question are:

Prepare journal entries to make the necessary corrections.

Calculate the correct profit for the year.

Calculate the profit margin.

Suggest two ways in which the trader could improve this ratio.

Calculate the trade receivables turnover.

Comment on your answer to this calculation.

Explain why the trader's return on capital employed is lower than that of a neighbouring business.

Identify two possible reasons for the change in the current ratio.

Each part of this question requires analysis.

TIP

The skill of analysis includes correction of errors and profit correction, more complicated calculation of ratios, interpretation of ratios and suggestions for improving various financial aspects of a business.

3

How to demonstrate analysis

It is essential to make sure you know what is required. If you need to do a calculation, use your knowledge to set out the required formula and use your understanding to select the relevant figures. If you need to comment on ratios or make suggestions for improving ratios in various situations, think carefully before you start writing: the answer must relate directly to the scenario described in the question and the ratios you have calculated. Simply listing possible solutions to a problem is not adequate: the answer must analyse the information in the question and make use of any calculations from a previous part of the answer.

1.4 Evaluation

You should be able to:

- interpret and evaluate accounting information and draw reasoned conclusions.

This is another skill which cannot be learned by rote. It requires a thorough appreciation of the other two skills and also develops with practice. This requires you to apply the skills of knowledge, understanding and analysis to a given scenario and to offer reasoned advice as to whether or not a certain course of action should be embarked upon.

How to recognise when evaluation is required

Command words requiring evaluation include:

advise, discuss, evaluate, examine, justify, recommend and summarise.

The following summarised question shows you how these command words can be used.

Example 1.3

A question provides a scenario about a trader needing to make decisions on certain matters which are detailed in the question.

The requirements of the question are:

Advise the trader whether or not he should reduce the rate of trade discount he allows to customers.

Discuss whether or not the trader should cease to sell on credit to his customers.

Recommend whether or not the trader should take a long-term loan to expand his business.

Each part of this question requires evaluation.

TIP

The skill of evaluation includes offering advice about the effects of a possible course of action or making recommendations about such a course of action.

How to demonstrate evaluation

Once again, read the question carefully and plan your answer before you start writing. You will need to be able to discuss the advantages and disadvantages of a course of action and to consider the implications of putting a plan into effect. Having outlined the points for and against, you are expected to make a recommendation on whether or not the course of action should be embarked upon and whether the plan should be put into effect.

This section of the Workbook provides advice on applying the skills of accounting to a given scenario. Example responses are given, along with tips for improving them. Full suggested answers for each question are provided at the end of the section.

Example 2.1

Question

Gary is a manufacturer. His financial year ends on 31 March. He provided the following information on 31 March 20–7:

		$
Inventories 1 April 20–6	Raw materials	33 200
	Work in progress	20 420
	Finished goods	49 740
Purchases	Raw materials	366 400
	Finished goods	11 350
Purchases returns of raw materials		3 800
Wages	Factory operatives	254 300
	Factory indirect wages	100 780
	Office and sales staff wages	93 130
General expenses	Factory	70 548
	Office	33 792
Factory machinery at cost		180 000
Office equipment at cost		34 000
Provision for depreciation of factory machinery		87 840
Provision for depreciation of office equipment		15 300

Additional information
1 At 31 March 20–7:

Inventories	Raw materials	33 520
	Work in progress	22 380
	Finished goods	46 960
Wages accrued	Factory operatives	1 620
	Office and sales staff	1 990

2 Depreciation is charged as follows:

Factory machinery at 20% per annum using the reducing balance method.

Office equipment at 15% per annum using the straight line method.

a Select the appropriate figures and prepare the manufacturing account for the year ended 31 March 20–7.

TIP

This question requires the skill of knowledge and understanding because it requires you to know and understand the principles of preparing a manufacturing account.

After the preparation of the manufacturing account, Gary's accountant prepared an income statement and a statement of financial position.

b i Define the term income statement.

ii Define the term statement of financial position.

iii State what is meant by capital.

TIP

This question requires the skill of knowledge and understanding because it requires you to know the meaning of three accounting terms.

7

The accountant calculated Gary's profit for the year ended 31 March 20–7 to be $39 600. It was then discovered that he had been provided with information which contained errors.

c Complete the following table to indicate the effect of correcting each error. Where an error does not affect the profit, place a tick (✔) in the 'No effect' column.

Error		Effect on profit of correcting the error		
		Increase $	Decrease $	No effect
1	One page of the sales journal had been overcast by $1 000.			
2	Sales to Asim, $1 560, had been debited to Aseem as $1 650.			
3	Returns from a credit customer, $3 110, had been recorded as credit sales.			
4	No adjustment had been made for $500 office insurance prepaid at 31 March 20–7.			

TIP

This question requires the skill of analysis, because it requires you to calculate the consequences of correcting errors.

Gary is considering purchasing new factory machines to replace the existing ones. The cost would be $140 000. He would have to take out a five-year bank loan for the full amount. Interest of 6% would have to be paid at the end of each year but he will not pay off the loan until the end of the period. Gary estimates that his annual operating profit should increase by $9 500.

d Advise Gary whether or not he should purchase the new machines. Justify your answer.

TIP

This question requires the skill of evaluation because it requires you to evaluate the advantages and disadvantages of a course of action and make a recommendation.

A student produced the following answer to Part a of this question

a

Gary
Manufacturing account for the year ended 31 March 20–7

	$	$
Opening inventory of raw materials		33 200
Purchases of raw materials		366 400
Purchases returns		(3 800)
Closing inventory of raw materials		(33 520)
		362 280
Direct factory wages		252 680
		614 960
Factory overheads		
Factory general expenses	70 548	
Indirect wages (100 780 + 93 140)	193 120	
Depreciation	87 840	351 508
		263 452
Opening work in progress	20 420	
Closing work in progress	(22 380)	(1 960)
		261 492

Tips on improving this answer

1 The cost of materials consumed, the prime cost and the production cost of goods completed should be labelled.

2 It is preferable to show the net purchases figure.

3 It is important to show every step in each calculation – the calculation of direct wages should be shown.

4 Only costs relating to the factory should be included in this account so office and sales staff wages should not be included.

5 It is preferable to state the name of the asset being depreciated.

6 Only the depreciation for the year should be included and not the accumulated depreciation from previous years.

7 It is important to remember that the account is adding together all the costs of manufacturing so the overheads should be added to the prime cost.

8 It is perfectly acceptable to show the work in progress in this manner, but students often do not make the correct adjustment for the net figure.

Exercise

See if you can prepare a manufacturing account which would be an improvement the above account.

When you have completed the account, you can compare it with the suggested version shown at the end of the section.

A student produced the following answer to Part b of this question

b i An income statement shows the income and expenses.

ii A statement of financial position shows the financial position of the business for the period.

iii Capital is the amount invested in the business at the start.

Tips on improving this answer

1 In part **i**: mention should be made of the time period covered by the statement and the purpose of preparing it.

2 In part **ii**: a statement of financial position does not cover a period of time. Mention should be made of exactly what this document shows.

3 In part **iii**: capital can be introduced at any point in the life of a business. The explanation should indicate who introduced this capital.

Exercise

See if you can prepare improved answers to the theory questions.

When you have completed your answers, you can compare them with the suggested answers shown at the end of the section.

A student produced the following answer to Part c of this question

	Error	Effect on profit of correcting the error		
c		Increase $	Decrease $	No effect
1	One page of the sales journal had been overcast by $1 000.		✓	
2	Sales to Asim, $1 560, had been debited to Aseem as $1 650.			90
3	Returns from a credit customer, $3 110, had been recorded as credit sales.		3 110	
4	No adjustment had been made for $500 office insurance prepaid at 31 March 20–7.	500		

Tips on improving this answer

1   The first two columns require an amount of money to be inserted. The last column requires only a tick not a sum of money.

2   Where sales returns have been entered as credit sales the profit will be affected by twice the amount of those returns.

3   In order to calculate the effect on profit of correcting an error it can be useful to draft a simple income statement and use that to see the effect of errors.

Exercise

See if you can complete the table in a way that would improve the above answer.

When you have completed your answer, you can compare it with the suggested version shown at the end of the section.

A student produced the following answer to Part d of this question

d   Gary would have to pay loan interest, but he estimates the profit will increase.

Tips on improving this answer

1   The advantages and disadvantages of the proposal should be considered.

2   In this case, it is possible to provide calculations which will form part of the advice.

3   A recommendation should be given on whether or not Gary should proceed with this proposal.

Exercise

See if you can produce an answer which would improve the above answer.

When you have completed your answer, you can compare it with a suggested answer shown at the end of the section.

Example 2.2

Question

Aurelie is a trader. Her book-keeper has recently left the business and Aurelie requires assistance with her financial records.

Aurelie maintains a petty cash book with an imprest amount of $200 which is restored on the first day of each month. The petty cash book has analysis columns for cleaning, office expenses, travel expenses and ledger accounts.

The following information is available for May 20–1:

May 1   Balance on petty cash book, $54.

Imprest restored from business bank account.

5   Paid train fare, $28.

9   An employee repaid $10 he had borrowed from petty cash in April.

13   Bought cleaning materials, $11.

18   Paid Wilma, a credit supplier, $42.

21   Paid office expenses, $13.

26   Paid taxi fare, $12.

30   Paid cleaner, $72.

a i Write up the petty cash book for May 20–1. Balance the book and bring down the balance on 1 June 20–1.

ii Write up the travel expenses account for May 20–1.

iii State how the entry in the ledger account column would be recorded in the ledger.

TIP

This question requires the skill of knowledge and understanding because it requires you to know and understand the principles of preparing a petty cash book and the necessary transfers to the ledger.

On 30 May 20–1, Aurelie's cash book showed an overdraft of $1 110. A comparison with the bank statement showed that the following items appeared in the cash book but did not appear on the bank statement:

	$
Cheques paid by Aurelie – William	380
George	410
Cheque received by Aurelie – Martha	530
Cash sales paid into bank	860

b Prepare a bank reconciliation statement at 30 May 20–1 to show the balance on the bank statement.

TIP

This question requires the skill of knowledge and understanding because it requires you to know the principles of bank reconciliation and to understand how to relate that knowledge to the scenario provided.

Aurelie's bank is offering $\frac{1}{2}$ % cash back on all monthly payments made by direct debit.
Aurelie pays both her telephone bill and her rates bill monthly by cheque.

c Advise Aurelie whether or not to arrange for these monthly payments to be made by direct debit.

TIP

This question requires the skill of evaluation because it requires you to evaluate the advantages and disadvantages of a course of action and make a recommendation.

A provision for doubtful debts has been maintained in Aurelie's ledger. The following is an extract from that account:

Provision for doubtful debts account								
Date	Details	Folio	$	Date	Details	Folio	$
20–1				20–0			
April 30	Income statement		20	May 1	Balance	b/d	260
	Balance	c/d	240				
			260				260
				20–1			
				May 1	Balance	b/d	240

Aurelie is considering discontinuing the provision for doubtful debts as she had not had to write off any debts as irrecoverable during the financial year ended on 30 April 20–1.

d i Explain **each** entry in the above account.

 ii Explain to Aurelie why she should continue to maintain a provision for doubtful debts.

TIP

Part **i** of this question requires the skill of knowledge and understanding because it requires you to know and understand the principles of double entry and apply them to a provision for doubtful debts account.

Part **ii** of this question requires the skill of analysis because it requires you to analyse the implications of discontinuing the provision of doubtful debts.

A student produced the following answer to Part a of this question

a i

Aurelie
Petty cash book

Total received $	Date	Details	Total paid $	Cleaning $	Office expenses $	Travel expenses $	Ledger accounts $
	20-1						
54	May 1	Balance b/d					
146		Bank					
	5	Train fare				28	
10	9	Employee					
	13	Cleaning		11			
	18	Credit supplier					42
	21	Office expenses			13		
	26	Taxi fare				12	
	30	Cleaning		72			
			178	83	13	40	42
		Balance c/d	32				
210			210				

ii

Aurelie
Travel expenses account

Date	Details	$	Date	Details	$
20-1					
May 5	Petty cash	28			
26	Petty cash	12			

iii The ledger accounts would have been debited with $42.

Tips on improving this answer

1 The individual payments should have been entered in the total column as well as the appropriate analysis column.

2 The details given for the transactions on 9 and 18 May are not adequate for posting to the appropriate ledger accounts.

3 The balance at the end of the month should have been brought down.

4 Only the total of the analysis columns is posted to the ledger accounts at the end of the month – not the individual transactions.

5 There is no ledger account with the title 'ledger accounts'. Any payments in the ledger account column will be debited to the accounts of the individual credit suppliers.

13

Exercise

See if you can prepare improved answers to this question.

When you have completed your answer, you can compare it with the suggested answer shown at the end of the section.

A student produced the following answer to Part b of this question

b

	Aurelie Bank reconciliation		
		$	$
Balance shown in cash book (overdraft)			1 110
William		380	
George		410	790
			(1 900)
Martha		530	
Cash sales		860	1 390
Balance shown on bank statement			(510)

Tips on improving this answer

1 The heading should give a correct title and the date to which the statement relates.

2 It is not adequate to simply write the names of the people to whom cheques were payable and from whom they were received: correct descriptions of amounts not credited and cheques not presented should be provided.

3 The student has made a fundamental error by treating the subtotals of $790 and $1 390 incorrectly: if the opening figure of $1 110 had been shown in brackets, this error may have been avoided.

Exercise

See if you can prepare an improved answer to this question.

When you have completed the account, you can compare it with the suggested answer shown at the end of the section.

A student produced the following answer to Part c of this question

c   This is a good idea – he should set up direct debits.

Tip on improving this answer

The advantages and disadvantages of the proposal should be considered before any recommendation is made.

> ### Exercise
>
> See if you can produce an improved answer for the above answer.
>
> When you have completed your answer, you can compare it with a suggested answer shown at the end of the section.

A student produced the following answer to Part d of this question

d   i   20–0 May 1   This is the balance of the account.
       20–1 April 30 This is what was transferred to the income statement.
                      This is the balance of the account.

   ii   Aurelie should continue to maintain a provision for doubtful debts as she will be ignoring some of the accounting principles if she does not.

Tips on improving this answer

The statements made in **d i** are true but do not explain the significance of each entry. Much more detail is required.

The statement made in **d ii** is true but much more detail is required. The particular principles should be named and explanations provided about how these principles relate to maintaining a provision for doubtful debts.

> ### Exercise
>
> See if you can produce an improved answer for the above answers.
>
> When you have completed your answers, you can compare them with a suggested answer shown at the end of the section.

Suggested answers

All exam-style questions and sample answers in this title have been written by the author.

Example 2.1

a

Gary		
Manufacturing account for the year ended 31 March 20-7		
	$	$
Cost of materials consumed		
Opening inventory of raw materials		33 200
Purchases of raw materials	366 400	
Purchases returns	3 800	362 600
		395 800
Closing inventory of raw materials		33 520
		362 280
Direct factory wages (254 300 + 1 620)		255 920
Prime cost		618 200
Factory overheads		
Factory general expenses	70 548	
Indirect wages	100 780	
Depreciation of factory machinery (20% × (180 000 – 87 840))	18 432	189 760
		807 960
Opening work in progress		20 420
		828 380
Closing work in progress		22 380
Production cost of goods completed		806 000

b i An income statement is used to calculate the profit for the period (usually one year) by comparing the revenues and the costs.

   ii A statement of financial position shows the assets, liabilities and capital of a business on a certain date.

   iii Capital represents the total resources provided by the owner of a business.

c

Error		Effect on profit of correcting the error		
		Increase $	Decrease $	No effect
1	One page of the sales journal had been overcast by $1 000.		1 000	
2	Sales to Asim, $1 560, had been debited to Aseem as $1 650.			✓
3	Returns from a credit customer, $3 110, had been recorded as credit sales.		6 220	
4	No adjustment had been made for $500 office insurance prepaid at 31 March 20-7.	500		

d Based on the estimates provided, interest of $8 400 per annum would have to be paid.

The profit for the year (i.e. after interest) is expected to increase by $1 100.

Will the cash be available to pay the annual interest?

Will the cash be available to repay the loan at the end of year 5?

What security will the bank require?

How reliable are the estimates?

Will there be other costs that have not been considered, such as retraining workers?

On the basis of the information provided, I recommend that Gary should not proceed with this proposal.

Example 2.2

a i

Aurelie
Petty cash book

Total received $	Date	Details	Total paid $	Cleaning $	Office expenses $	Travel expenses $	Ledger accounts $
	20–1						
54	May 1	Balance b/d					
146		Bank					
	5	Train fare	28			28	
	9	Loan repayment					
10							
	13	Cleaning	11	11			
	18	Wilma	42				42
	21	Office expenses	13		13		
	26	Taxi fare	12			12	
	30	Cleaning	72	72			
			178	83	13	40	42
		Balance c/d	32				
210			210				
	20–1						
32	June 1	Balance b/d					

ii

Aurelie
Travel expenses account

Date	Details	$	Date	Details	$
20–1					
May 30	Petty cash	40			

a iii The account of Wilma in the purchases ledger would have been debited with $42.

b

Aurelie		
Bank reconciliation statement at 30 May 20–1		
	$	$
Balance shown in cash book		(1 110)
Cheques not yet presented		
William	380	
George	410	790
		(320)
Amounts not yet credited		
Martha	530	
Cash sales	860	1 390
Balance shown on bank statement		(1 710)

c The total paid each month would be less than at present because of the 'cash back' scheme.

Payments would be made automatically so no action is required from Aurelie.

Aurelie cannot fall behind with the payments.

Amounts will be paid irrespective of the balance at bank – so may fall into overdraft, which would not necessarily happen if Aurelie paid by cheque as she could control the dates of payment.

Aurelie may have higher bank charges (but these may be offset by the 'cash back' scheme).

There is greater security than sending a cheque through the post.

On the information supplied, I recommend that Aurelie arranges for these payments to be made by direct debit.

d i 20–0 May 1   This represents the provision for doubtful debts at the start of the financial year.

       20–1 April 30   This represents the surplus provision for doubtful debts (the difference between the opening and closing provision) which is transferred to the credit side of the income statement as other income.

       20–1 April 30/   This is the balance of the account which is carried down from the end of the
       20–1 May 1   financial year to the start of the next financial year. It represents the provision for doubtful debts at the start of the next financial year.

ii Aurelie should continue to maintain a provision for doubtful debts. If this is not done, she will not be applying the following accounting principles:

Consistency: once a policy is decided upon it should be applied consistently unless there is a good reason to change.

Prudence: losses should always be anticipated to avoid overstating profits.

Accruals: the amount of sales for which Aurelie is unlikely to be paid should be regarded as expenses of the year in which those sales were made.

This section of the Workbook offers suggestions on the steps required when answering accounting questions.

Always think carefully and read both the data given and the requirements, to make sure that you understand what is needed.

It is useful to show calculations even where these are not specifically required by a question and it is a good idea to provide clearly labelled workings.

Below are three example questions. They are accompanied by suggested answers and an outline of the stages involved in preparing those answers.

All exam-style questions and sample answers in this title have been written by the author.

Example 3.1

Chao is a business advisor. He provided the following trial balance at 31 July 20–8:

	$		$
Salaries	52 000	Fees from clients	120 000
Rates and insurance	7 100	Provision for doubtful debts	880
Advertising	9 400	Provision for depreciation	
Motor expenses	3 100	of equipment	980
General office expenses	17 236	Provision for depreciation	
Premises at cost	60 000	of motor vehicles	5 250
Equipment at cost	9 800	Loan (5% pa) repayable	
Motor vehicles at cost	12 000	31 December 20–9	20 000
Trade receivables	31 000	Capital	79 000
Drawings	42 000	Bank overdraft	17 526
	243 636		243 636

The following additional information is also provided:

1 At 31 July 20–8:

- salaries accrued amounted to $2 100

- rates prepaid amounted to $210

- one year's interest was accrued on the loan.

2 The equipment is being depreciated at 10% per annum using the straight line method.

The motor vehicles are being depreciated at 20% per annum using the reducing balance method.

3 Irrecoverable debts of $300 are to be written off.

The provision for doubtful debts is to be adjusted to 2% of the remaining trade receivables.

a Prepare the income statement of Chao for the year ended 31 July 20–8.

b Prepare the statement of financial position of Chao at 31 July 20–8.

> **TIP**
> This question requires the skill of knowledge and understanding.

Answer

a

Chao		
Income statement for the year ended 31 July 20–8		
	$	$
Fees from clients		120 000
Add Reduction in provision for doubtful debts (880 – 614)		266
		120 266
Less Salaries (52 000 + 2 100)	54 100	
Rates and insurance (7 100 – 210)	6 890	
Advertising	9 400	
Motor expenses	3 100	
General office expenses	17 236	
Irrecoverable debts	300	
Depreciation of equipment (10% × 9 800)	980	
Depreciation of motor vehicles (20% × (12 000 – 5 250))	1 350	93 356
Profit from operations		26 910
Less Loan interest		1 000
Profit for the year		25 910

b

	Chao		
Statement of financial position at 31 July 20–8			
	$	$	$
	Cost	Accumulated depreciation	Net book value
Assets			
Non-current assets			
Premises	60 000		60 000
Equipment	9 800	1 960	7 840
Motor vehicles	12 000	6 600	5 400
	81 800	8 560	73 240
Current assets			
Trade receivables		30 700	
Less Provision for doubtful debts		614	30 086
Other receivables			210
			30 296
Total assets			103 536
Capital and liabilities			
Capital			
Opening balance			79 000
Plus Profit for the year			25 910
			104 910
Less Drawings			42 000
			62 910
Non-current liabilities			
Loan (repayable 31 December 20–9)			20 000
Current liabilities			
Other payables			3 100
Bank overdraft			17 526
			20 626
Total capital and liabilities			103 536

The stages in producing the answer

1   Go through the trial balance and the accompanying notes and label all the items.

Put a label 'IS' against anything which will be used in the income statement.

Put a label 'FP' against anything which will be used in the statement of financial position.

Remember that anything in the trial balance is used once in a set of financial statements and any notes to a trial balance are used twice.

The items should be labelled as follows:

		$			$
IS	Salaries	52 000	IS	Fees from clients	120 000
IS	Rates and insurance	7 100	IS	Provision for doubtful debts	880
IS	Advertising	9 400	FP	Provision for depreciation	
IS	Motor expenses	3 100		of equipment	980
IS	General office expenses	17 236	FP	Provision for depreciation	
FP	Premises at cost	60 000		of motor vehicles	5 250
FP	Equipment at cost	9 800	FP	Loan (5% pa) repayable	
FP	Motor vehicles at cost	12 000		31 December 20–9	20 000
FP	Trade receivables	31 000	FP	Capital	79 000
FP	Drawings	42 000	FP	Bank overdraft	17 526
		243 636			243 636

1   At 31 July 20–8:

IS FP   salaries accrued amounted to $2 100

IS FP   rates prepaid amounted to $210

IS FP   one year's interest is accrued on the loan.

IS FP   2   The equipment is to be depreciated at 10% per annum using the straight line method.

IS FP   The motor vehicles are to be depreciated at 20% per annum using the reducing balance method.

IS FP   3   Irrecoverable debts of $300 are to be written off.

IS FP   The provision for doubtful debts is to be adjusted to 2% of the remaining trade receivables.

2   Prepare the income statement.

Tick off the items as they are used to ensure that nothing is omitted.

The trial balance and accompanying notes should now appear as follows:

		$			$
✓ IS	Salaries	52 000	✓ IS	Fees from clients	120 000
✓ IS	Rates and insurance	7 100	✓ IS	Provision for doubtful debts	880
✓ IS	Advertising	9 400	FP	Provision for depreciation	
✓ IS	Motor expenses	3 100		of equipment	980
✓ IS	General office expenses	17 236	FP	Provision for depreciation	
FP	Premises at cost	60 000		of motor vehicles	5 250
FP	Equipment at cost	9 800	FP	Loan (5% pa) repayable	
FP	Motor vehicles at cost	12 000		31 December 20–9	20 000
FP	Trade receivables	31 000	FP	Capital	79 000
FP	Drawings	42 000	FP	Bank overdraft	17 526
		243 636			243 636

1 At 31 July 20–8:

✓ **IS FP**   salaries accrued amounted to $2 100

✓ **IS FP**   rates prepaid amounted to $210

✓ **IS FP**   one year's interest is accrued on the loan.

✓ **IS FP** 2 The equipment is to be depreciated at 10% per annum using the straight line method.

✓ **IS FP**   The motor vehicles are to be depreciated at 20% per annum using the reducing balance method.

✓ **IS FP** 3 Irrecoverable debts of $300 are to be written off.

✓ **IS FP**   The provision for doubtful debts is to be adjusted to 2% of the remaining trade receivables.

Remember that the exiting provision for doubtful debts only appears in the income statement as part of the calculation of the amount which is surplus to requirements.

3 Prepare the statement of financial position.

Tick off the items as they are used to ensure that nothing is omitted.

The trial balance and accompanying notes should now appear as follows:

		$			$
✓ **IS**	Salaries	52 000	✓ **IS**	Fees from clients	120 000
✓ **IS**	Rates and insurance	7 100	✓ **IS**	Provision for doubtful debts	880
✓ **IS**	Advertising	9 400	✓ **FP**	Provision for depreciation	
✓ **IS**	Motor expenses	3 100		of equipment	980
✓ **IS**	General office expenses	17 236	✓ **FP**	Provision for depreciation	
✓ **FP**	Premises at cost	60 000		of motor vehicles	5 250
✓ **FP**	Equipment at cost	9 800	✓ **FP**	Loan (5% pa) repayable	
✓ **FP**	Motor vehicles at cost	12 000		31 December 20–9	20 000
✓ **FP**	Trade receivables	31 000	✓ **FP**	Capital	79 000
✓ **FP**	Drawings	42 000	✓ **FP**	Bank overdraft	17 526
		243 636			243 636

1 At 31 July 20–8:

✓ ✓ **IS FP**   salaries accrued amounted to $2 100

✓ ✓ **IS FP**   rates prepaid amounted to $210

✓ ✓ **IS FP**   one year's interest is accrued on the loan.

✓ ✓ **IS FP** 2 The equipment is to be depreciated at 10% per annum using the straight line method.

✓ ✓ **IS FP**   The motor vehicles are to be depreciated at 20% per annum using the reducing balance method.

✓ ✓ **IS FP** 3 Irrecoverable debts of $300 are to be written off.

✓ ✓ **IS FP**   The provision for doubtful debts is to be adjusted to 2% of the remaining trade receivables.

Example 3.2

At the end of her financial year on 31 May 20–9, the totals of Rita's trial balance failed to balance. The total of the debit side was $98 730 and the total of the credit side was $99 176. She entered the difference in a suspense account and prepared a draft income statement. The profit for the year was calculated at $9 366.

The following errors were then discovered:

1 An invoice for goods sold on credit to Waqas had been entered in the sales journal as $1 100 instead of $110.

2 The purchases returns journal had been overcast by $100.

3 A new motor vehicle was purchased on 30 May 20–9. The total cost, $12 650, which included $340 for fuel and insurance, had been debited to the motor vehicles account. No depreciation is required for the motor vehicle for the year ended 31 May 20–9.

4 The total of the discount received column in the cash book, $82, had been debited to the discount allowed account in the ledger.

5 The balance of the petty cash book, $50, had been omitted from the trial balance.

6 Brian is both a supplier and a customer. Sales, $230, on credit to Brian had been credited to the account of Brian in the purchases ledger.

    a Prepare journal entries to correct errors 1–6 above. Narratives are not required.

    b Write up the suspense account showing all the necessary corrections. Start with the balance arising from the difference on the trial balance.

    c Prepare a statement to show the corrected profit for the year ended 31 May 20–9.

TIP
This question requires the skill of analysis.

Answer

a

Rita		
Journal		

	Debit $	Credit $
1 Sales	990	
Waqas		990
2 Purchases returns	100	
Suspense		100
3 Motor vehicle expenses	340	
Motor vehicle		340
4 Suspense	164	
Discount allowed		82
Discount received		82
5 –		
Suspense		50
6 Brian (purchases ledger)	230	
Brian (sales ledger)	230	
Suspense		460

b

Rita							
Suspense account							

Date	Details	Folio	$	Date	Details	Folio	$
20–9				20–9			
May 31	Difference on			May 31	Purchases returns		100
	trial balance		446		Petty cash		50
	Discount allowed		82		Brian		
	Discount received		82		(purchases ledger)		230
					Brian		
					(sales ledger)		230
			610				610

c

	Rita		
	Statement of corrected profit for the year ended 31 May 20–9		
		$	$
Profit for the year			9 366
Add Discount received understated		82	
Discount allowed overstated		82	164
			9 530
Less Sales overstated		990	
Purchases returns overcast		100	
Motor vehicle expenses understated		340	1 430
Corrected profit for the year			8 100

The stages in producing the answer

a   Journal entries

1   An invoice for goods sold on credit to Waqas had been entered in the sales journal as $1 100 instead of $110.

The entries made were as follows:

There was an error in the sales journal. The incorrect figure would have been posted to the account of Waqas and the total sales transferred to the sales account would also be incorrect. Ignoring any other items, the entries made were:

Sales account		Waqas account	
	1 100	1 100	

The entries that should have been made are:

Sales account		Waqas account	
	100	100	

The entries needed to correct the error are:

Sales account		Waqas account	
990			990

A journal entry can now be made debiting the sales account and crediting Waqas' account with $990. This will result in a net entry of $110 on the correct side of each account.

The trial balance totals are not affected so an entry in the suspense account is not needed.

2   The purchases returns journal had been overcast by $100.

The entry made were as follows:

The incorrect figure for the total of the purchases returns journal would have been credited to the purchases returns account. Ignoring any other items, the entry made was:

Purchases returns account	
990	

There are no errors on the debit side as only the total of the purchases journal is incorrect.

The entries needed to correct the error are:

Purchases returns account	
100	

Suspense account	
	100

Because this error was on one side of the ledger only, it affected the balancing of the trial balance. An entry in the suspense account must be made to make a double entry for the debit of $100.

A journal entry can now be made debiting the purchases returns account and crediting the suspense account with $100.

3   **A new motor vehicle was purchased on 30 May 20–9. The total cost, $12 650, which included $340 for fuel and insurance, had been debited to the motor vehicles account.**

No depreciation is required for the motor vehicle for the year ended 31 May 20–9.

The entry made was:

Motor vehicle account	
12 650	

The total cost was debited to the motor vehicle expenses account.

The entries that should have been made are:

Motor vehicle account	
12 310	

Motor vehicle expenses account	
340	

The entries needed to correct the error are:

Motor vehicle account	
	340

Motor vehicle expenses account	
340	

A journal entry can now be made debiting the motor vehicle account and crediting the motor vehicle expenses account with $340.

The trial balance totals are not affected so an entry in the suspense account is not needed.

4   **The total of the discount received column in the cash book, $82, had been debited to the discount allowed account in the ledger.**

Ignoring any other items, the entry made was:

Discount allowed account	
82	

The entry that should have been made is:

Discount received account	
	82

There were no errors in the individual purchases ledger accounts as only the total of the column was treated incorrectly.

The entries needed to correct the error are:

Discount allowed account	
	82

Discount received account	
	82

Suspense account	
164	

Because this error resulted in an amount being debited that should have been credited, it affected the balancing of the trial balance. An entry in the suspense account of $164 must be made to make a double entry for the two credits of $82.

A journal entry can now be made debiting the suspense account with $164 and crediting both the discount allowed account and the discount received account with $82.

5 **The balance of the petty cash book, $50, had been omitted from the trial balance.**

No errors of double entry were made. The only error made was to omit a balance from the trial balance.

The entries needed to correct this error:

Insert the petty cash balance in the debit column of the trial balance.

This error affected the balancing of the trial balance. An entry in the suspense account must be made.

Suspense account	
	50

A single-sided journal entry can now be made crediting the suspense account with $50.

6 **Brian is both a supplier and a customer. Sales, $230, on credit to Brian had been credited to the account of Brian in the purchases ledger.**

Ignoring any other items, the entry was:

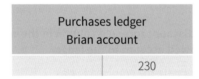

Purchases ledger Brian account	
	230

The entry that should have been made is:

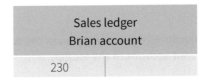

Sales ledger
Brian account

230	

The entries needed to correct the error are:

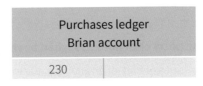

Purchases ledger
Brian account

230	

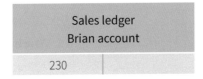

Sales ledger
Brian account

230	

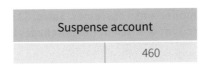

Suspense account

	460

Because this error resulted in an amount being credited that should have been debited, it affected the balancing of the trial balance. An entry in the suspense account must be made of $460 to make a double entry for the two debits of $230.

A journal entry can now be made by debiting both Brian's account in the purchases ledger and Brian's account in the sales ledger with $230 and crediting the suspense account with $460.

b   Suspense account

Calculate the difference between the totals of the trial balance. Enter this figure on the debit side of the suspense account.

Refer back to the calculations and the journal entries and make the appropriate entries in the suspense account. Total the account.

c   Statement of corrected profit for the year

Consider each error:

1   **An invoice for goods sold on credit to Waqas had been entered in the sales journal as $1 100 instead of $110.**

Correcting this error reduces the sales. This means that the profit will also reduce. This item should be deducted from the profit for the year.

2   **The purchases returns journal had been overcast by $100.**

Correcting this error reduces the purchases returns, which in turn increases the net purchases. This means that the profit will reduce.

This item should be deducted from the profit for the year.

3   **A new motor vehicle was purchased on 30 May 20–9. The total cost, $12 650, which included $340 for fuel and insurance, had been debited to the motor vehicles account.**

No depreciation is required for the motor vehicle for the year ended 31 May 20–9.

Correcting this error increases the motor vehicle expenses. This means that the profit will reduce.

This item should be deducted from the profit for the year.

29

(If the motor vehicle had been purchased earlier in the year and depreciation was required, this would have to be adjusted as the calculation would have been made on $12 650 rather than the correct figure of $12 310.)

4 The total of the discount received column in the cash book, $82, had been debited to the discount allowed account in the ledger.

Correcting this error increases the discount received. This means that the profit will also increase. The correction also reduces the discount allowed. This means that the profit will increase.

This means that both of these items should be added to the profit for the year.

5 The balance of the petty cash book, $50, had been omitted from the trial balance.

Correcting this error does not affect any items in the income statement so the profit is not affected.

6 Brian is both a supplier and a customer. Sales, $230, on credit to Brian had been credited to the account of Brian in the purchases ledger.

Correcting this error does not affect any items in the income statement so the profit is not affected.

Write down the profit for the year shown in the draft statement.

Add the items which increase the profit for the year.

Deduct the items which reduce the profit for the year.

Calculate the corrected profit for the year.

Example 3.3

Ashok started business on 1 January 20–2 with a capital of $26 000. This consisted of equipment, $9 000, a motor vehicle, $12 000, and the remainder in cash which was paid into a business bank account.

Ashok did not maintain any accounting records, but was able to provide the following information at the end of his first month of trading on 31 January 20–2:

		$
1	Cheques received and paid into the bank	
	Credit customers	4 000
2	Payments by cheque	
	Credit suppliers	4 200
	Wages	800
	Rent and rates	300
	Insurance	95
	Office cash	400
3	Cash receipts	
	Bank	400
	Cash sales	2 400
4	Cash payments	
	Cash purchases	500
	General expenses	890

5 Ashok failed to calculate the value of his inventory on 31 January 20–2. All goods were sold at a mark-up of 50%.

6 During the month of January 20–2:

Ashok took goods, at cost, for his own use	300
Sales returns amounted to	240
Purchases returns amounted to	950
Irrecoverable debts written off amounted to	160

7 At 31 January 20–2:

Trade receivables amounted to	2 110
Trade payables amounted to	2 650

8 Ashok decided to depreciate his non-current assets as follows:

Equipment at 10% per annum on cost

Motor vehicle at 20% per annum on cost.

a Prepare the income statement of Ashok for the month ended 31 January 20–2.

b Prepare the statement of affairs of Ashok at 31 January 20–2.

TIP
This question requires the skill of knowledge and understanding.

Answer

a

Ashok
Income statement for the month ended 31 January 20–2

	$	$	$
Revenue		8 910	
Less Sales returns		240	8 670
Less Cost of sales			
Purchases	8 300		
Less Purchases returns	950		
	7 350		
Less Goods for own use	300	7 050	
Less Closing inventory		1 270	5 780
Gross profit			2 890
Less Wages		800	
Rent and rates		300	
Insurance		95	
General expenses		890	
Irrecoverable debts		160	
Depreciation of equipment		75	
Depreciation of motor vehicle		200	2 520
Profit for the month			370

b

Ashok			
Statement of affairs at 31 January 20–2			
	$	$	$
	Cost	Accumulated depreciation	Net book value
Assets			
Non-current assets			
Equipment	9 000	75	8 925
Motor vehicle	12 000	200	11 800
	21 000	275	20 725
Current assets			
Inventory			1 270
Trade receivables			2 110
Bank			3 205
Cash			1 410
			7 995
Total assets			28 720
Capital and liabilities			
Capital			
Opening balance			26 000
Plus Profit for the month			370
			26 370
Less Drawings			300
			26 070
Current liabilities			
Trade payables			2 650
Total capital and liabilities			28 720

The stages in producing the answer

a Income statement

1 Calculate the revenue.

				Total trade receivables account			
Date	Details	Folio	$	Date	Details	Folio	$
20–2				20–2			
Jan 31	Sales*		6510	Jan 31	Bank		4000
					Returns		240
					Irrecoverable debts		160
					Balance	c/d	2110
			6510				6510
20–2							
Feb 1	Balance	b/d	2110				

	$
Total revenue	
Credit sales	6510
Cash sales	2400
	8910

2 Calculate the purchases.

				Total trade payables account			
Date	Details	Folio	$	Date	Details	Folio	$
20–2				20–2			
Jan 31	Bank		4200	Jan 31	Purchases*		7800
	Returns		950				
	Balance	c/d	2650				
			7800				7800
				20–2			
				Feb 1	Balance	b/d	2650

	$
Total purchases	
Credit purchases	7800
Cash purchases	500
	8300

3 Enter the revenue and purchases in the income statement.

   Remember to also enter the sales returns, purchases returns and goods taken for own use.

   Calculate and enter the gross profit. The mark-up is 50%, so the gross profit will be $\frac{50}{150}$ × the revenue, i.e. $\frac{1}{3}$ of the revenue.

   Working 'backwards', the missing figure of closing inventory can be inserted.

4 Calculate the depreciation. Remember that statements are for one month only.

Equipment $10\% \times \$9\,000 \times \frac{1}{12} = \$75$

Motor vehicle $20\% \times \$12\,000 \times \frac{1}{12} = \$200$

5 Enter the expenses in the income statement.

Remember to include the general expenses paid in cash and the irrecoverable debts.

Calculate the profit for the month.

b Statement of affairs

1   Calculate the bank balance.

Bank account							
Date	Details	Folio	$	Date	Details	Folio	$
20–2				20–2			
Jan 1	Capital		5 000	Jan 31	Total payments		5 795
31	Total receipts		4 000		Balance	c/d	3 205
			9 000				9 000
20–2							
Feb 1	Balance	b/d	3 205				

2   Calculate the cash balance.

Cash account							
Date	Details	Folio	$	Date	Details	Folio	$
20–2				20–2			
Jan 31	Total receipts		2 800	Jan 31	Total payments		1 390
					Balance	c/d	1 410
			2 800				2 800
20–2							
Feb 1	Balance	b/d	1 410				

3   Prepare the statement of affairs.

Templates for the preparation of financial statements

This section provides outlines of the main types of financial statements for different types of trading and non-trading organisations.

The idea is not to learn the form of presentation by rote, but rather to understand the reasons why these accounting statements are presented in these formats. However, some students find it helpful to make use of a pro forma accounting statement, especially at the beginning of their studies.

The items shown within the accounting statements are intended to be representative of the types of items which would appear in each section – they are not intended to be definitive lists. For example, the expenses shown in the income statement may not apply to every business, and some businesses will have other types of expenses.

Similarly, the non-current assets shown in the statements of financial position may not apply to every business and some businesses will have other types of non-current assets.

Example 4.1

Financial statements of a trading business owned by one person

Sole trader			
Income statement for the year ended			
	$	$	$
Revenue			XXXX
Less Sales returns			XXXX
			XXXX
Less Cost of sales			
Opening inventory		XXXX	
Purchases	XXXX		
Less Purchases returns	XXXX		
	XXXX		
Less Goods for own use	XXXX		
	XXXX		
Carriage inwards	XXXX	XXXX	
		XXXX	
Less Closing inventory		XXXX	XXXX
Gross Profit			XXXX
Add other income			
Discount received			XXXX
Rent receivable			XXXX
Commission receivable			XXXX
*Profit on disposal of non-current assets			XXXX
**Reduction in provision for doubtful debts			XXXX
			XXXX
Less Expenses			
Wages and salaries		XXXX	
Office expenses		XXXX	
Rent and rates		XXXX	
Insurance		XXXX	
Motor vehicle expenses		XXXX	
Selling expenses		XXXX	
*Loss on disposal of non-current assets		XXXX	
Irrecoverable debts		XXXX	
**Provision for doubtful debts		XXXX	
Depreciation of fixtures and fittings		XXXX	
Depreciation of office equipment		XXXX	
Depreciation of motor vehicles		XXXX	XXXX
Profit from operations			XXXX
Less Loan interest			XXXX
***Profit for the year			XXXX

* If only one asset was sold during the year, only one of these items will appear.

** If the provision reduces, the surplus amount is added to the gross profit; if the provision increases, the amount required is included in the expenses.

*** If the expenses exceed the total income, the resulting figure is described as a loss for the year.

	$	$	$
Sole trader			
Statement of financial position at			
	Cost	Accumulated depreciation	Net book value
Assets			
Non-current assets			
Land and buildings	XXXX		XXXX
Fixtures and fittings	XXXX	XXXX	XXXX
Office equipment	XXXX	XXXX	XXXX
Motor vehicles	XXXX	XXXX	XXXX
	XXXX	XXXX	XXXX
Current assets			
Inventory			XXXX
Trade receivables		XXXX	
Less Provision for doubtful debts		XXXX	XXXX
Other receivables			XXXX
Other receivables (accrued income)			XXXX
* Bank			XXXX
Cash			XXXX
Petty cash			XXXX
			XXXX
Total assets			XXXX
Capital and liabilities			
Capital			
Opening balance			XXXX
** Plus Profit for the year			XXXX
			XXXX
Less Drawings			XXXX
			XXXX
Non-current liabilities			
Loan			XXXX
Current liabilities			
Trade payables			XXXX
Other payables			XXXX
Prepaid income			XXXX
* Bank overdraft			XXXX
			XXXX
Total capital and liabilities			XXXX

* If the business has only one bank account, only one of these items will appear.
** If there is a loss for the year, this will be deducted rather than added.

Example 4.2

Financial statements of a service business owned by one person

A service business is one which does not buy and sell goods. It is not necessary to prepare a trading section of an income statement at the end of the financial year as the business does not earn a gross profit. Only a profit and loss section of an income statement is required which is similar to that of a trading business, excluding the gross profit. The format of the statement of financial position is exactly the same as that of a trading business.

Sole trader		
Income statement for the year ended		
	$	$
Fees receivable		XXXX
Commission receivable		XXXX
Rent receivable		XXXX
Discount received		XXXX
*Profit on disposal of non-current assets		XXXX
**Reduction in provision for doubtful debts		XXXX
		XXXX
Less Expenses		
Wages and salaries	XXXX	
Office expenses	XXXX	
Rent and rates	XXXX	
Insurance	XXXX	
Motor vehicle expenses	XXXX	
Selling expenses	XXXX	
*Loss on disposal of non-current assets	XXXX	
Irrecoverable debts	XXXX	
**Provision for doubtful debts	XXXX	
Depreciation of fixtures and fittings	XXXX	
Depreciation of office equipment	XXXX	
Depreciation of motor vehicles	XXXX	XXXX
Profit from operations		XXXX
Less Loan interest		XXXX
***Profit for the year		XXXX

* If only one asset was sold during the year, only one of these items will appear.
** If the provision reduces, the surplus amount is added to the total income; if the provision increases, the amount required is included in the expenses.
*** If the expenses exceed the income, the resulting figure is described as a loss for the year.

The statement of financial position of a service business of a sole trader is presented in exactly the same format as the statement of financial position of a trading business of a sole trader.

Example 4.3

Financial statements of a partnership business

The income statement of a partnership follows the same format as that of a sole trader. The only difference is that interest on a loan from a partner may be included with any other loan interest in the final part of the income statement.

It is necessary to prepare an appropriation account to show the distribution of the profit for the year between the partners.

Partnership				
Profit and loss appropriation account for the year ended				
		$	$	$
Profit for the year				XXXX
Add Interest on drawings	Partner A		XXXX	
	Partner B		XXXX	XXXX
Less Interest on capital	Partner A	XXXX		
	Partner B	XXXX	XXXX	
Partner's salary	Partner A		XXXX	XXXX
* Profit shares	Partner A		XXXX	
	Partner B		XXXX	XXXX

*Residual profit is shared in the ratio stated in the partnership agreement.

The assets section of the statement of financial position of a partnership follows the same format as that of a sole trader. The sections for non-current liabilities and current liabilities also follow the same format as that of a sole trader. The capital section has to be modified so that it shows the capital and current account of each partner.

Where the full details of the partners' current accounts are not required, the capital section of a partnership statement of financial position could be presented as follows:

Partnership			
Extract from statement of financial positon at			
	$	$	$
	Partner A	Partner B	Total
Capital accounts	XXXX	XXXX	XXXX
* Current accounts	XXXX	XXXX	XXXX
	XXXX	XXXX	XXXX

* Where a balance is a debit balance, it is shown in brackets and deducted rather than added.

Where full details of the current accounts are required, the capital section of a partnership statement of financial position could be presented as follows:

Partnership			
Extract from statement of financial positon at			
	$	$	$
Capital accounts	XXXX	XXXX	XXXX
Current accounts			
*Opening balance	XXXX	XXXX	
Interest on capital	XXXX	XXXX	
Partner's salary	XXXX		
**Profit shares	XXXX	XXXX	
	XXXX	XXXX	
Less Drawings	XXXX	XXXX	
Interest on drawings	XXXX	XXXX	
	XXXX	XXXX	
	XXXX	XXXX	XXXX
			XXXX

* Where a balance is a debit balance, it is shown in brackets and deducted rather than added.
** Where there is a loss to share out, it is shown in brackets and deducted rather than added.

Example 4.4

Financial statements of a limited company

The income statement of a limited company follows the same format as that of a sole trader.

One difference is that directors' remuneration may appear in the expenses in the income statement. Another difference is that the finance costs may include debenture interest and dividends on redeemable preference shares.

It is necessary for a limited company to prepare a statement of changes in equity. This summarises the changes during the year to the ordinary share capital, non-redeemable preference share capital, retained earnings and general reserve.

Limited company Statement of changes in equity for the year ended	$ Ordinary share capital	$ General reserve	$ Retained earnings	$ Total
Balance at xxxxxxxxxx (start of year)	xxxx	xxxx	xxxx	xxxx
Share issue	xxxx			xxxx
Profit for the year			xxxx	xxxx
Dividend paid (final dividend for previous year)			(xxxx)	xxxx
Dividend paid (interim dividend for current year)			(xxxx)	(xxxx)
Transfer to general reserve		xxxx	(xxxx)	
Balance at xxxxxxxxx (close of year)	xxxx	xxxx	xxxx	xxxx

If there had been non-redeemable preference shares, an extra column would have been added. The dividends actually paid on these shares would have been recorded in a similar way to the dividends paid on ordinary shares.

The assets section of the statement of financial position of a limited company follows the same format as that of a sole trader. The sections for non-current liabilities and current liabilities also follow the same format as that of a sole trader, with debentures and redeemable preference shares being included in the non-current liabilities. The capital section has to be modified so that it shows the share capital and reserves.

Limited company Extract from statement of financial positon at	$
Equity and liabilities	
Equity	
Ordinary share capital	xxxx
General reserve	xxxx
Retained earnings	xxxx
	xxxx

Any non-redeemable preference shares would also be included in this section.

The total of the second section of the statement of financial position would be labelled 'Total equity and liabilities'.

Example 4.5

Financial statements of a manufacturing business

Where a business manufactures goods it is necessary to prepare a manufacturing account to show the calculation of the cost of manufacture. This follows the same format irrespective of the ownership of the business.

Sole trader or partnership or limited company			
Manufacturing account for the year ended			
	$	$	$
Cost of material consumed			
Opening inventory of raw material		XXXX	
Purchases of raw material		XXXX	
Carriage on raw material		XXXX	
		XXXX	
Less Closing inventory of raw material		XXXX	XXXX
Direct wages			XXXX
Direct expenses			XXXX
Prime cost			XXXX
Add Factory overheads			
Indirect wages		XXXX	
Factory rent and rates		XXXX	
Factory insurance		XXXX	
Factory fuel and power		XXXX	
Factory general expenses		XXXX	
Depreciation of factory machinery		XXXX	XXXX
			XXXX
Add Opening work in progress			XXXX
			XXXX
Less Closing work in progress			XXXX
Production cost of goods completed			XXXX

The income statement of a manufacturing business follows the same format as that of any other form of business. The only difference is that the trading section will include the production cost of goods completed.

Sole trader or partnership or limited company		
Income statement for the year ended		
	$	$
Revenue		XXXX
Less Cost of sales		
Opening inventory of finished goods	XXXX	
Cost of production	XXXX	
Purchases of finished goods	XXXX	
	XXXX	
Less Closing inventory of finished goods	XXXX	XXXX
Gross profit		XXXX

The profit and loss section of the income statement will include only office, selling and financial expenses.

The statement of financial position of a manufacturing business follows the same format as that of any other form of business. The only difference is that there may be three inventories rather than one.

Example 4.6

Financial statements of a non-trading organisation

The treasurer of a non-trading organisation usually prepares a summary of the cash book which is known as a receipts and payments account. This shows all money received on the debit side and all money paid out on the credit side and is balanced in the same way as a cash account.

A trading section of an income statement may be prepared if the organisation operates a shop or café, etc. where goods are bought and sold. This is very similar to the trading section of an income statement of a business.

Non-trading organisation Shop income statement for the year ended			
	$	$	$
Revenue			XXXX
Less Cost of sales			
Opening inventory		XXXX	
Purchases	XXXX		
Less Purchases returns	XXXX		
	XXXX		
Carriage inwards	XXXX	XXXX	
		XXXX	
Less Closing inventory		XXXX	
Cost of sales		XXXX	
Shop expenses	XXXX		
Wages of shop assistant	XXXX		
Shop rent and rates	XXXX		
Depreciation of shop fittings	XXXX	XXXX	XXXX
Profit on shop (transferred to income and expenditure account)			XXXX

The treasurer will prepare the equivalent of the profit and loss section of an income statement of a business. This is known as an income and expenditure account.
It follows the same format as a profit and loss section of an income statement.
The expenses of the organisation are deducted from the income. The resulting figure is referred to as a surplus or deficit rather than a profit or loss.

Non-trading organisation		
Income and expenditure account for the year ended		
	$	$
Income		
Subscriptions		XXXX
Profit on shop		XXXX
Competition – Entrance fees	XXXX	
Less expenses	XXXX	XXXX
Interest received		XXXX
*Profit on disposal of non-current assets		XXXX
		XXXX
Expenditure		
General expenses	XXXX	
Rates and insurance	XXXX	
Repairs and maintenance	XXXX	
Loan interest	XXXX	
*Loss on disposal of non-current assets	XXXX	
Depreciation of equipment	XXXX	XXXX
**Surplus for the year		XXXX

* If only one asset was sold during the year, only one of these items will appear.
** If the expenditure exceeds the income, the resulting figure is described as a deficit.

The assets section of the statement of financial affairs of a non-trading organisation follows the same format as that of a sole trader. The sections for non-current liabilities and current liabilities also follow the same format as that of a sole trader. The capital section has to be modified so that it shows the accumulated fund and the surplus or deficit.

Non-trading organisation		
Extract from statement of financial position at		
	$	$
Accumulated fund and liabilities		
Accumulated fund		
Opening balance		XXXXX
*Plus Surplus for the year		XXXXX
		XXXXX

*If there is a deficit, this will be deducted rather than added.

This section of the Workbook contains multiple choice and structured questions that are directly linked to the topics covered in the Coursebook. You can tackle a section of the book when you have completed that section of the Coursebook or you can choose to work through all the sections towards the end of your course. All multiple choice and structured questions, along with their answers, have been written by the author.

Section 1 (*Chapters 1–5 of the Coursebook*)

Multiple choice questions

1 Said, a retailer, purchased goods, $400, from a wholesaler and paid in cash. How did this affect Said's total assets and total liabilities?

	Effect on total assets	$	Effect on total liabilities	$
A	increase	400	increase	400
B	increase	400	no effect	
C	no effect		increase	400
D	no effect		no effect	

2 Feng provided the following information:

	$
Office equipment	11 920
Cash at bank	4 210
Trade payables	9 760
Trade receivables	8 430
Inventory	10 610
Loan to employee	1 000

How much was Feng's capital?

A $24 410　　　B $26 410　　　C $27 070　　　D $29 070

3 Why should the owner of a business prepare financial statements at the end of each financial year?

A to calculate the amount owed to trade payables

B to calculate the bank balance at the year-end

C to calculate the profit or loss for the year

D to calculate the total amount spent during the year.

4 On 1 June, Bekele purchased goods on credit from Phayo. On 8 June, some of these goods were returned. How did Phayo record the transactions of 8 June?

	Account debited	Account credited
A	Bekele	purchases returns
B	Bekele	sales returns
C	purchases returns	Bekele
D	sales returns	Bekele

5 Mark transferred his private motor vehicle to his business. How did he record this?

	Account debited	Account credited
A	capital	motor vehicle
B	drawings	motor vehicle
C	motor vehicle	capital
D	motor vehicle	drawings

6 Omar's tenant, Seth, overpaid his rent by $10, which Omar refunded in cash. How would this refund be recorded in Seth's books?

	Account debited	Account credited
A	cash	rent payable
B	cash	rent receivable
C	rent receivable	cash
D	rent payable	cash

7 What may appear on the credit side of a trial balance?

   A carriage outwards   **C** motor vehicles

   B discount received   **D** sales returns

8 A food retailer purchased office equipment on credit from XY Supplies. This was credited to the account of XY and debited to the purchases account.

What type of error was made?

   A commission   **B** original entry   **C** principle   **D** reversal

9 The total of the debit column of a trial balance was $1 000 more than the total of the credit column. Which error caused this?

   A K Moses was debited with $500 paid to K Moss

   B The purchase of office equipment, $1 000, had not been recorded

   C The sales account was overcast by $1 000

   D Purchases returns, $500, had been debited to the sales returns account.

10 Which transaction is recorded by means of a contra entry?

   A cash withdrawn from bank for owner's personal expenses

   B cash withdrawn from bank to restore petty cash imprest

   C office cash paid into the business bank account

   D office cash used to pay for business expenses.

11 Wilma allowed a customer cash discount.

What did the customer do to earn this discount?

   A introduced a new customer

   B paid his account in cash

   C paid his account within a stated time

   D purchased a large quantity of goods.

12 Karl returned goods to Kenny, a credit supplier. How did Kenny record this transaction?

	Nominal (general ledger)	Sales ledger
A	credit Karl account	debit sales returns account
B	credit sales returns account	debit Karl account
C	debit Karl account	credit sales returns account
D	debit sales returns account	credit Karl

13 What is an advantage of the imprest system of petty cash?

    A   It ensures that fraud cannot take place

    B   Petty cash expenditure can be controlled

    C   Petty cash vouchers are not required

    D   The amount reimbursed is the same each month.

14 A petty cash book has an imprest amount of $100 which is restored on the last day of each month. During August, the petty cash payments totalled $86. A loan from petty cash, $20, to a member of staff in July was repaid on 29 August. The imprest was restored on 31 August.

How much was shown for petty cash in the statement of financial position prepared at close of business on 31 August?

    A $14   **B** $34   **C** $66   **D** $100

15 A business maintains a petty cash book with an imprest of $50, which is restored on the first day of each month.

On 31 March, there was $13.40 in the petty cash box and vouchers totalling $36.60.

How much did the petty cashier receive from the chief cashier on 1 April?

    A $13.40   **B** $23 20   **C** $36.60   **D** $50.00

Structured questions

1   Explain the difference between book-keeping and accounting.

2 **a**   State the formula for the accounting equation.

     b   Fill in the blanks in the following table:

	Capital $	Assets $	Liabilities $
i		50 000	15 000
ii	140 000		52 000
iii	45 000	68 000	
iv		99 000	27 000

3 Indicate whether **each** of the following is an asset or a liability of Anna who owns a general store. The first one has been completed as an example.

	Item	Asset	Liability
a	Fittings	✓	
b	Cash		
c	Inventory of goods		
d	Trade payables		
e	Trade receivables		
f	Motor vehicles		
g	Loan to employee		

TIP

This question requires the skill of knowledge and understanding. You need to know what is meant by the terms 'assets' and' liabilities' and to understand how to separate items into these two categories.

4 State how **each** of the following transactions affect the assets and liabilities of Mahesh who owns a factory. The first one has been completed as an example.

	Transaction	Effect on assets		Effect on liabilities
a	Bought goods for cash	Cash	Decrease	No effect
		Inventory	Increase	
b	Bought machine on credit			
c	Paid credit supplier by cheque			
d	Made a cash loan to employee			
e	Received a long term bank loan			

5 The statement of financial position of Mary on 1 January 20–9 is shown below.

Mary				
Statement of financial position at 1 January 20–9				
Assets	$	Liabilities		$
Premises	100 000	Capital		158 000
Fixtures	30 000	Trade payables		12 000
Inventory	18 000			
Trade receivables	13 000			
Bank	9 000			
	170 000			170 000

49

On 2 January 20–9, the following transactions took place:

Bought goods, $1 500, on credit.

A credit customer paid $500 by cheque.

Mary invested a further $10 000 by cheque.

Additional fixtures, $1 000, were bought on credit.

Prepare the statement of financial position of Mary on 2 January 20–9 after the above transactions have taken place.

TIP

This question requires the skill of knowledge and understanding. You need to know what a statement of financial position includes and you need to understand the effect of transactions on the items within the statement.

6 Kumar is a trader. On 1 August 20–8 his statement of financial position was as follows:

Kumar
Statement of financial position at 1 August 20–8

Assets	$	Liabilities	$
Machinery	55 000	Capital	80 000
Equipment	18 000	Loan	20 000
Motor vehicles	15 000	Trade payables	9 200
Inventory	9 500		
Trade receivables	6 500		
Bank	5 200		
	109 200		109 200

On 2 August 20–8, the following transactions took place:

Paid a credit supplier $2 100 by cheque.

A credit customer paid $100 in cash.

Purchased goods, $1 500, and paid by cheque.

Borrowed a further $10 000 and purchased an additional motor vehicle.

Prepare the statement of financial position of Kumar on 2 August 20–8 after the above transactions have taken place.

7 Jonny is thinking of starting a business.

a Explain to him how accounting records are an important source of information for the operating of the business.

b Explain why it is important that the profit or loss of the business is measured at regular intervals.

8 For each of the following transactions, insert the name of the account to be debited and the name of the account to be credited.

Transaction	Account to be debited	Account to be credited
a Paid rent by cheque		
b Bought goods for cash		
c Paid cash for carriage on goods bought		
d Bought equipment on credit from WR Stores		
e Sold goods on credit to Jones		
f Jones returned goods		
g The owner took goods for his own use		

9 Raminder provided the following information for March 20–9:

		$
March 1	Balance of cash	100
	Balance at bank	2 750
4	Received cheque from Wahid, a credit customer	280
9	Paid office expenses in cash	22
13	Received a loan from AB Loans by cheque	5 000
18	Purchased equipment and paid by cheque	4 500
24	Received commission by cheque	150
28	Paid Sabena, a credit supplier, by cheque	330
31	Cash sales	840
	Raminder took cash for personal use	200

Record the above transactions in Raminder's cash account and bank account. Balance the accounts on 31 March and bring down the balances on 1 April 20–9.

10 Mona started a business on 1 January 20–4. The following are her transactions for the first two weeks of trading:

January 1	Capital, $20 000, was paid into a business bank account.
	Paid rent, $500, by cheque.
2	Bought goods, $3 300, on credit from Mohamed.
4	Returned goods, $100, to Mohamed.
7	Sold goods, $1 700, on credit to Aswan Traders.
9	Received $120 commission in cash.
10	Paid Mohamed $3 000 by cheque on account.
12	Aswan Traders paid $1 000 by cheque on account.
13	Paid office expenses in cash $20.
14	Cash sales, $1 500.
	Cash withdrawn for personal use, $500.

Enter the above transactions in the ledger of Mona. Balance the cash account, the bank account and the accounts of Mohamed and Aswan Traders on 14 January and bring down the balances on 15 January 20–4.

TIP

This question requires the skill of knowledge and understanding. You need to know the principles of double entry and you need to understand how to apply that knowledge to various business transactions.

11 a From the following information, write up the account of Sanele in the books of Thomas for the month of July 20–1. Prepare the account in the three column running balance format:

July 1   Sanele owed Thomas $450.

       6   Sanele purchased goods, $1 200, on credit from Thomas.

      10   Sanele returned goods, $50, to Thomas.

      14   Sanele paid $250 to Thomas in cash.

      20   Sanele purchased goods, $590, on credit from Thomas.

      26   Sanele paid $1 000 by cheque to Thomas.

 b   State **one** advantage of using the three column running balance format for ledger accounts.

12 Jason started a business on 1 April 20–5. His transactions for the first month of trading were as follows:

April 1   Jason introduced capital of $40 000. Of this, $1 000 was in cash. The remainder was paid into the business bank account.

       2   Purchased premises, $25 000, by cheque.

       4   Purchased goods, $9 500, on credit from Lynne.

       6   Paid operating expenses, $250, in cash.

       9   Cash sales, $320.

      12   Sold goods, $1 460, on credit to Paul.

           Paid $10, in cash, for carriage on sales.

      15   Paul returned goods, $120.

      20   Jason took goods, $100, for his own use.

      24   Paid Lynne $8 000, on account, by cheque.

      27   Paul paid the amount outstanding by cheque.

      28   Received a long term loan, $10 000, by cheque, from ABC Finance.

      30   Paid assistant's wages in cash, $200.

Enter the above transactions in the ledger of Jason. Balance the cash account, the bank account and the accounts of Lynne and Paul on 30 April and bring down the balances on 1 May 20–5.

13 The following accounts appeared in the ledger of Akinola. Explain **each** entry in **each** of the accounts and also state where the double entry for **each** entry will be found.

a

Akinola
Anwar account

Date	Details	Folio	$	Date	Details	Folio	$
20–6				20–6			
Mar 1	Balance	b/d	250	Mar 12	Returns		30
9	Sales		870	18	Bank		800
				31	Balance	c/d	290
			1 120				1 120
20–6							
April 1	Balance	b/d	290				

b

Akinola
Drawings account

Date	Details	Folio	$	Date	Details	Folio	$
20–6				20–6			
Mar 10	Bank		100	Mar 31	Capital		365
28	Purchases		265				
			365				365

TIP

This question requires the skill of knowledge and understanding. You need to know the principles of double entry and you need to understand how these have been applied in the preparation of these accounts.

14 a State **two** uses of a trial balance.

b Name and explain **two** errors which a trial balance will not reveal.

c Explain which of the following errors would be revealed by a trial balance. Give a reason for your answer.

Error 1 Goods sold on credit to Appiah, $950, were recorded in the books as $590.

Error 2 Goods sold on credit to Appiah, $600, were omitted from Appiah's account.

Error 3 Goods sold on credit to Appiah, $720, were omitted from the books.

TIP

This question requires the skill of knowledge and understanding. You need to know how a trial balance can be used and how it may be affected by errors. You also need to understand the effect that certain errors may have on the balancing of a trial balance.

53

15 The following balances were extracted from the books of Peter on 31 October 20–2:

	$
Cash	600
Bank overdraft	10 500
Equipment	18 200
Fixtures and fittings	6 100
Trade receivables	12 400
Trade payables	13 600
Purchases	48 600
Sales	66 200
Sales returns	3 300
Wages	21 400
Office expenses	4 700
Carriage inwards	900
Operating expenses	4 000
Drawings	12 500
Capital	?

Prepare Peter's trial balance at 31 October 20–2, showing his capital account balance.

16 An inexperienced book-keeper prepared the following trial balance of Maria. The book-keeper placed various balances in the wrong column.

	$	$
Premises		60 000
Fixtures and fittings	13 500	
Inventory 1 January 20–4		9 500
Trade receivables		14 200
Trade payables	9 800	
Cash at bank		2 300
Loan from XY Finance	5 000	
Purchases		36 100
Sales	45 900	
Sales returns		1 400
Rent and rates	4 700	
Wages	12 300	
Operating expenses	2 500	
Carriage outwards		2 600
Capital (balancing figure)	32 400	
	126 100	126 100

Prepare Maria's amended trial balance at 31 December 20–4, showing the correct capital account balance.

17 John is a trader. He has little knowledge of accounting, but attempted to prepare a trial balance at the end of his financial year. The trial balance he prepared is shown below.

John Trial balance for the year ended 30 November 20–8		
	Debit $	Credit $
Purchases		174 900
Sales	246 500	
Carriage inwards	5 650	
Carriage outwards		4 210
Bank overdraft	14 500	
Operating expenses		3 600
Equipment	5 700	
Motor vehicles	10 400	
Salaries		62 590
Trade receivables		21 610
Trade payables	16 440	
Rent and rates	7 990	
Insurance		3 200
Inventory 1 December 20–7	14 850	
Loan to employee		1 000
Capital (balancing figure)		50 920
	322 030	322 030

In addition to the obvious errors in the above trial balance, the following errors have also been discovered:

1   Drawings, $4 100, have been omitted from the trial balance.

2   A cheque, $90, paid to Chan, a creditor, has been debited to Chen's account.

3   Both the salaries account and the purchases account have been undercast by $1 000.

4   No entry has been made for operating expenses, $2 150, paid by cheque.

a   State how **each** of the above errors will affect the trial balance. Give a reason for your answer in each case.

b   Prepare an amended trial balance for John at 30 November 20–8.

18 a State **one** reason why the ledger is often divided into specialised areas.

b Complete the following table and indicate in which ledger of a trader the following accounts would be recorded. The first has been completed for you as an example.

	Account	Sales ledger	Purchases ledger	Nominal ledger
i	Wages			✓
ii	Sales			
iii	Inventory			
iv	Hassan, a debtor			
v	Khan, a creditor			
vi	Drawings			

TIP

This question requires the skill of knowledge and understanding. You need to know the reasons for dividing the ledger into sections. You also need to understand what types of account will appear in each section of the ledger.

19 The balances on Anjori's cash and bank accounts on 1 May 20–9 were:

	$
Cash	200
Bank	4 960

The following transactions took place during the month:

May	4	Paid Western Stores $2 120 by bank transfer.
	9	Received a cheque, $1 310, from C Wright.
	13	Cash sales, $950.
	15	Paid $40 in cash for carriage on sales.
	19	Paid $900 cash into bank.
	22	Anjori withdrew $500 from the bank for her own use.
	26	Paid insurance, $1 420, by direct debit.
	30	Purchased a motor vehicle, $5 500, and paid by cheque.

a Record the transactions for May in Anjori's cash book and bring down the balances on 1 June 20–9.

b Explain the meaning of the word 'contra' when used in connection with cash books.

c Explain why it is **not** possible to have a credit balance brought down on a cash account.

d State whether the cash balance and the bank balance in Anjori's cash book at the end of May 20–9 represent assets or liabilities.

20 Vikram's financial year ends on 30 November. The balances in his cash book on 1 November 20–3 were as follows:

	$
Cash	135
Bank overdraft	3 150

The following transactions took place in November 20–3:

November 7   Received a cheque, $50, from High Street Stores.

14   The bank returned High Street Stores' cheque as dishonoured.

17   Cash sales, $1 670, paid directly into the bank.

20   Paid Marine Traders $936 by bank transfer after deducting $24 cash discount.

23   Paid a cheque to Seafresh Foods in settlement of their account of $750 less 2% discount.

26   Received a cheque from Valley Stores in settlement of their debt of $200 less 4% cash discount.

29   Withdrew $1 000 cash from bank for business use.

30   Paid wages, $860, in cash.

a Record the transactions for November 20–3 in Vikram's three column cash book. Balance the cash and bank columns and bring down the balances on 1 December 20–3.

b Explain why a trader may grant cash discount.

c Calculate the percentage of cash discount Vikram deducted when he paid Marine Traders on 20 November.

d Explain the entry that should be made in the ledger on 26 November in respect of the discount allowed.

e Explain the treatment of the totals of the discount columns in the cash book at the end of each month.

21 Sara started a business on 1 July 20–7. On that date, she paid $20 000 into a business bank account. She decided to maintain a three column cash book and to divide her ledger into three sections – sales, purchases and nominal.

Sara's transactions for the first month of trading were as follows:

July 3   Withdrew $200 from the bank for office use.

5   Paid rent, $350, by cheque.

7   Purchased goods, $1 500, on credit from BeeLine & Co.

10   Received long term loan, $6 000, by bank transfer from HiFinance.

13   Bought motor vehicle, $5 900, and paid by bank transfer.

17   Paid motor expenses, $150, in cash.

20   Sold goods, $2 100, on credit to Honey Farm.

22   Paid BeeLine & Co a cheque to settle their account less 3% cash discount.

25   Honey Farm returned goods, $100.

28   Purchased goods, $930, on credit from BeeLine & Co.

       Paid $20 in cash for carriage on purchases.

31   Received a cheque from Honey Farm for $1 950 in full settlement of their account.

57

a Enter the above transactions in the books of Sara. Balance the cash and bank columns in the cash book at 31 July and bring down the balances on 1 August.

b Transfer the totals of the discount columns to the relevant accounts in the nominal ledger.

c Balance the accounts in the sales and purchases ledgers, as required.

d Draw up a trial balance at 31 July 20–7.

Sara's landlord has asked her to consider paying the rent by monthly direct debit instead of by a monthly cheque.

e Advise Sara on whether or not she should start to pay her rent by a monthly direct debit.

TIP

Parts **a** to **d** of this question require the skill of knowledge and understanding. You need to understand the principles of double entry and trial balances and you need to understand how to apply those principles to a given situation.

Part **e** of this question requires the skill of evaluation. You need to evaluate the information provided and draw a reasoned conclusion.

22 Mirza is a trader. On 1 November 20–2 he had the following balances on his books.

		$	
Cash book – Cash		400	Dr
Bank		5 900	Dr
Sales ledger – Redfern Traders		500	
Purchases ledger – Square Tiles Co		2 300	
Nominal ledger – Capital		44 000	
Machinery		30 000	
Inventory		3 500	
Fixtures and fittings		6 000	

a Enter the above balances in the appropriate accounts on 1 November 20–2.

The following transactions took place during November 20–2:

November 3 Sold goods, $350, on credit to Southern Traders.

7 Bought goods, $1 600, on credit from Square Tiles Co.

10 Received commission, $210, in cash.

15 Returned goods, $230, to Square Tiles Co.

17 Paid for machine repairs, $570, by cheque.

18 Received a cheque, $500, from Redfern Traders.

20 Paid a cheque to Square Tiles Co for the amount owing on 1 November less 2% cash discount.

22 Received $340 by bank transfer from Southern Traders in full settlement of the amount due.

25 Cash sales, $1 620.

28 The bank returned Redfern Traders' cheque as dishonoured.

30 Paid all the cash into the bank except $500.

b Enter the above transactions in the books of Mirza. Balance the cash book and personal accounts as necessary on 30 November 20–2 and bring down the balances on 1 December 20–2. Transfer the totals of the discount columns to the nominal ledger on 30 November 20–2.

c Draw up a trial balance on 30 November 20–2.

23 On 1 February 20–9, Eniola, a sole trader, decided to open a petty cash book using the imprest system. She decided to use four analysis columns – office expenses, postages, refreshments and ledger accounts. The monthly imprest was to be $200.

Her transactions for February 20–9 were as follows:

			$
February	1	Transfer from bank account.	200
	3	Paid office expenses.	15
	4	Bought postage stamps.	10
	9	Purchased refreshments.	21
	12	Paid Central Stores, a credit supplier.	30
	14	Paid for parcel postage.	5
	16	Paid office expenses.	11
	21	Received from employee for personal postage cost.	2
	26	Paid High Street Trading Co.	19

a Explain what is meant by the imprest system of petty cash.

b State **one** advantage of using the imprest system of petty cash.

c Write up Eniola's petty cash book for February 20–9. Balance the book on 28 February and bring down the balance on 1 March. Make the entry on 1 March to restore the petty cash imprest amount from the bank.

> **TIP**
> This question requires the skill of knowledge and understanding. You need to know the imprest system and understand its advantages. You also need to know the principles of entering transactions in a petty cash book and understand how to apply those principles to a given situation.

24 Rashid is a sole trader who keeps an analysed petty cash book using the imprest system. The imprest amount is $100.

His transactions for the week beginning 1 October 20–1 were as follows:

			$
October	1	Balance of petty cash.	21
		Petty cash restored to imprest amount in cash.	
	2	Paid bus fares.	4
	3	Bought envelopes.	3
	4	Bought postage stamps.	20
	5	Paid Ali, a credit supplier.	12
		Paid taxi fare.	8
	6	Paid cleaner's wages.	30
	7	Paid Zafar, a credit supplier.	10

a Write up Rashid's petty cash book for the week ending 7 October 20–1. Use four analysis columns – travel, postages and stationery, cleaning, and ledger accounts. Balance the book on 7 October and bring down the balance on 8 October. Make an entry on 8 October to restore the petty cash to the imprest amount.

b Post the analysis columns to the appropriate accounts in Rashid's ledgers.

c State where the double entry will be found for the restoration of the imprest amount on 1 October.

d State the section of Rashid's statement of financial position at 7 October 20–1 in which petty cash would appear. State the amount of petty cash which would appear.

25 Kate is a trader. She maintains a cash book and a petty cash book. All receipts are banked each day. All payments are made by cheque unless under $15, when they are paid from petty cash.

The following information is available for the week beginning 25 July 20–6:

			$
Balances			
July	25	Bank overdraft	750
		Petty cash imprest amount	60
Receipts			
July	26	Bank transfer from North Star Co to pay their account of $1 200 less a cash discount of $2\frac{1}{2}$ %	
		Cheque from Western Traders	25
Payments			
July	27	General expenses	10
	28	Motor expenses	59
	29	Oriental Fashions in settlement of $1 950 owing	1 911
	30	General expenses	8
		Train fare	9
		Copy paper	12
		Southlands & Co	13

The following additional information is also available:

July 30 The bank dishonoured the cheque received from Western Traders.

a Write up the petty cash book for the week ending 31 July 20–6. The book should have four analysis columns – general expenses, travel expenses, postages and stationery, and ledger accounts.

Balance the book on 30 July 20–6 and restore the imprest on 31 July 20–6.

b Write up the cash book for the week ending 31 July 20–6. Balance the book on 31 July after the restoration of the petty cash imprest.

26 Liphie is a sole trader. She has several employees including a cashier. It has been suggested that it would be a good idea to start using a petty cash book in addition to the three column cash book maintained by the cashier.

Advise Liphie on whether or not it would be of benefit for the business to have a petty cash book.

TIP
This question requires the skill of evaluation. You need to be able to evaluate the information provided and draw a reasoned conclusion.

Section 2 (*Chapters 6–7 of the Coursebook*)

Multiple choice questions

1 What is the name of the document that summarises the customer's transactions for the month?

A credit note   **B** debit note   **C** invoice   **D** statement of account

2 On 1 June, Samir sold goods on credit to Faisal. Some of the goods were returned on 8 June.

In what order would Samir and Faisal exchange documents in June?

A credit note, debit note, invoice   **C** invoice, credit note, debit note
B debit note, credit note, invoice   **D** invoice, debit note, credit note

3 Which statement about a debit note is correct?

A It is sent to the supplier to request a reduction in the amount of an invoice
B It is sent to the customer to request a reduction in the amount of an invoice
C The customer records it in the purchases returns journal
D The supplier records it in the sales returns journal.

4 Heidi's sales returns journal shows the following:

	Goods $	Trade discount $	Net price $
March 31 Total for month	4400	880	3520

What entry would be made in the sales returns amount on 31 March?

A credit $3520   **B** credit $4400   **C** debit $3520   **D** debit $4400

5 Which document is used to write up the purchases returns journal?

A credit note issued   **C** debit note issued

B credit note received   **D** debit note received

6 Which statements about trade discount are correct?

1 It is an allowance for buying in bulk.

2 It is an allowance for prompt payment.

3 It is shown as a deduction on an invoice.

4 It is shown as an expense in an income statement.

A 1 only   **B** 2 only   **C** 1 and 3   **D** 2 and 4

Structured questions

1 Explain the purpose of a statement of account.

2 Neither the supplier nor the customer makes entries in their accounting records when a debit note is issued. Explain why.

3 Tracey is a credit customer of Lydia.

The following documents are issued in February 20–8: cheque, receipt, invoice, statement of account, debit note and credit note.

Complete the table below listing the documents in the order in which they would be issued. Name the person who would issue each document.

	Document in order of issue	Name of person issuing the document
a		
b		
c		
d		
e		
f		

4 The following account appeared in the ledger of Simon;

Paul account							
Date	Details	Folio	$	Date	Details	Folio	$
20–6				20–6			
Jan 7	Purchases returns		120	Jan 4	Purchases		520
21	Bank		390				
	Discount		10				
			520				520

a Complete the following table by placing a tick (✓) against **each** document that Simon would have used as a source of information in preparing the above account.

Document	✓
Cheque	
Credit note	
Debit note	
Invoice	
Statement of account	

b Select one of the documents you have not ticked and explain why this was not used in the preparation of the ledger account.

> **!**
>
> **TIP**
>
> This question requires the skill of knowledge and understanding. You need to know the purpose of each of the business documents listed. You also need to understand why some, but not all, of these documents are used to make entries in the ledger.

5 Study the invoice shown below and answer the questions that follow.

Sales Invoice
Building Supplies
Lobastse Road
Francistown

P Onamusi
Mokolodi Road
Kgale   13 April 20–1

Quantity	Description	Price per unit $		Total $
25 metres	Floorboards	1.60 per metre		40.00
50 metres	Treated timber posts	2.20 per metre	**i** ☐	
6	Doors	**ii** ☐		300.00
			iii ☐	
	Less 20% trade discount		**iv** ☐	
			v ☐	

Terms: $2\frac{1}{2}$% cash **vi** ☐ if paid within 30 days

a State the name of the business issuing the invoice.

b Calculate and write down the missing amounts at **i** to **v**.

c State the word which is missing at **vi**.

d Explain why the supplier has allowed the customer trade discount.

e State the amount of the cheque which was sent to pay for the goods on 4 May 20–1.

f Complete the following table to show how the invoice would be recorded in the books of both the supplier and the customer:

	Account to be debited	Account to be credited
i Supplier's books		
ii Customer's books		

6 Study the business document shown below and answer the questions that follow.

i....................... note

Building Supplies
Lobastse Road
Francistown

J Moyo
Unit 2 Industrial Estate
Mahalapye   17 November 20–5

Quantity	Description	Unit price		Total $
40	Floor tiles Design XR234	$2	**ii**	
	Less 25% trade discount		**iii**	
			iv	

Reason for return – Damage

a State the word which is missing at **i**.

b Calculate and write down the missing amounts at **ii** to **iv**.

c Name the document which J Moyo may have sent to Building Supplies which resulted in the above document being issued.

d Explain why it is necessary to deduct trade discount on the above document.

On 1 November 20–6, J Moyo owed Building Supplies $330. He purchased further goods, $280, on credit on 10 November. After the above document was issued on 17 November, there were no further transactions in November. J Moyo settled his account by cheque on 30 November after deducting a cash discount of 2%.

e Prepare the account of J Moyo for November 20–6 as it would appear in the ledger of Building Supplies.

f i State the ledger of J Moyo in which the account of Building Supplies would appear.

ii State the ledger of Building Supplies in which the account of J Moyo would appear.

TIP

This question requires the skill of knowledge and understanding. You need to know the purpose and content of debit and credit notes. You need to understand how to record transactions in the ledger and you also need to understand the division of the ledger.

7 List **five** books of original entry.

8 State **two** advantages of maintaining a sales journal.

9 During October, Susie listed her credit purchases in her purchases journal and totalled the journal at the end of the month. State what entries will be made in Susie's ledgers at the end of October.

10 Ben is a sole trader who buys and sells on credit. He maintains a full set of accounting records. He provided the following information for May 20–2:

Date	Transaction	Supplier	$
May 4	Goods bought	Pet Products Ltd	560
12	Goods bought	Cosy Canines	634
16	Goods returned	Cosy Canines	28
21	Goods bought	Pampered Pets & Co	422
27	Goods returned	Pampered Pets & Co	12

a Enter the above transactions in Ben's purchases journal and purchases returns journal. Total the journals on 31 May 20–2.

b Make the necessary entries in the following accounts in Ben's ledgers – purchases account, purchases returns account, Pet Products Ltd account, Cosy Canines account and Pampered Pets & Co account.

c Complete the following table to indicate in which of Ben's ledgers **each** of the following accounts would appear:

Account	Ledger
Purchases account	
Purchases returns account	
Pet Products Ltd account	
Cosy Canines account	
Pampered Pets & Co account	

> **TIP**
> This question requires the skill of knowledge and understanding. You need to know the double entry system and division of the ledger. You also need to understand how to transfer information from the books of prime entry to the ledger.

11 Nahida is a trader who keeps a full set of accounting records. Her transactions for June 20–9 included the following:

Sales journal			
Date	Details	$	$
20–9			
June 10	London Road Stores		
	Goods		310
21	West End Fashions		
	Goods	350	
	Trade discount	70	280
30	Total for month		590

Sales returns journal			
Date	Details	$	$
20–9			
June 27	West End Fashions		
	Goods	100	
	Trade discount	20	80
30	Total for month		80

Cash book (debit side)			
		Discount allowed $	Cash $	Bank $
20–9				
June 14	London Road Stores	6		234
28	West End Fashions	5		195
30	Sales		2 120	

On 1 June, there was a debit balance of $240 on London Road Stores' account.

a Write up the accounts of London Road Stores and West End Fashions as they would appear in Nahida's sales ledger for the month of June 20–9. Balance or total the accounts, as necessary.

b Write up the sales account and the sales returns account as they would appear in Nahida's general ledger for the month of June 20–9.

On 29 June, an invoice was issued to London Road Stores for $330. This was not entered in the accounting records.

c Explain how this error would affect the current assets in Nahida's statement of financial position on 30 June 20–9.

d Complete the following table to show the business document and the book of prime entry that would be used for the following transactions:

Transaction	Document used by Nahida	Nahida's book of prime entry	Document used by Coco	Coco's book of prime entry
Goods sold on credit by Coco to Nahida				
Goods returned by Nahida to Coco				

> **TIP**
>
> Parts **a**, **b** and **d** of this question require the skill of knowledge and understanding. You need to know the sources of information for the books of prime entry and how the entries in these books are recorded in the ledger. You also need to understand the double entry system of book-keeping.
>
> Part **c** requires the skill of analysis. You need to analyse the effect of the error on the current assets.

Section 3 (*Chapters 8–13 of the Coursebook*)

Multiple choice questions

1 Which item is included when calculating the gross profit?

  A carriage inwards

  B carriage outwards

  C discount allowed

  D discount received

2 A trader provided the following information at the end of her financial year:

	$
Gross profit	35 200
Operating expenses	17 744
Loan interest payable	5 000
Commission receivable	1 475

What was the profit from operations?

  A $12 456   **B** $13 931   **C** $17 456   **D** $18 931

3 Sales returns were omitted from an income statement. What was the effect of this error?

| | Gross profit | | Profit for the year | | |
	Overstated	Understated	Overstated	Understated	No effect
A	✓		✓		
B	✓				✓
C		✓		✓	
D		✓			✓

4 What are assets?

A items that are expected to be turned into cash within one year
B items that are owned by or owed by a business
C items that are owned by or owed to a business
D items that are purchases for long-term use within a business.

5 Raja provided the following information:

	$
Non-current assets	29 500
Inventory	5 780
Petty cash	100
Bank overdraft	3 460
Trade payables	4 170
Trade receivables	5 030
Loan to employee	200

How much was Raja's capital?

A $31 260   B $32 580   C $32 880   D $32 980

6 On 1 January 20–7 Mona had a bank overdraft. On that date, she obtained a loan, $10 000, repayable on 1 December 20–7, and she purchased a motor vehicle, $12 000, paying by bank transfer.

How did these transactions affect the liabilities and current assets?

	Non-current liabilities		Current liabilities		Current assets	
A	increase	$10 000	increase	$2 000	no effect	
B	increase	$10 000	no effect		decrease	$2 000
C	no effect		increase	$10 000	decrease	$2 000
D	no effect		increase	$12 000	no effect	

7 The value to a business of a highly skilled manager is not recorded in the accounting records.

Which accounting principle is being applied?

A business entity   C money measurement
B materiality   D prudence

8 How should inventory be valued?

    A at cost price plus selling expenses

    B at selling price less selling expenses

    C at the higher of cost and net realisable value

    D at the lower of cost and net realisable value

9 What are examples of capital expenditure for a business selling and repairing motor cars?

    1 purchase of motor cars for re-sale

    2 purchase of new breakdown truck

    3 purchase of spare parts for motor cars

    4 purchase of tools for mechanics' use.

    A 1 and 3   **B** 1 and 4   **C** 2 and 3   **D** 2 and 4

10 When preparing the financial statements at the end of the financial year, no adjustment was made for insurance prepaid.

    What was the effect of this error?

	Profit for the year	Current assets
A	overstated	overstated
B	overstated	understated
C	understated	overstated
D	understated	understated

11 Rates outstanding at the end of the financial year are recorded as an accrued expense at the start of the next financial year.

    Which accounting principle is being applied?

    A duality   **C** money measurement

    B matching   **D** prudence

12 At the end of Abhay's financial year, a tenant had prepaid one month's rent.

    What adjustment for this will Abhay need to make in the financial statements?

	Income statement		Statement of financial position	
	Increase income	Decrease income	Increase current assets	Increase current liabilities
A	✓		✓	
B	✓			✓
C		✓	✓	
D		✓		✓

13 Rashida purchased a machine for $5 600. She sold it six years later for $500. At that date, the provision for depreciation had a credit balance of $5 040.

    What entry was made in the income statement?

    A credit $60   **B** debit $60   **C** credit $560   **D** debit $560

14 Which statements about the reducing balance method of depreciation are correct?

1   The depreciation charge is calculated on the original cost price of the asset.

2   The depreciation charge is calculated on the book value at the start of the year.

3   The same amount of depreciation is charged each year.

4   The same percentage rate of depreciation is used each year.

A   1 and 2   **B**   1 and 3   **C**   2 and 4   **D**   3 and 4

15 Jack depreciates his office machinery at 20% per annum based on the cost of machinery held at the year-end. Jack calculated the annual depreciation at $840. He then discovered that $200 debited to the machinery account related to machinery repairs.

How did this error affect the profit for the year?

A   overstated by $40   **C**   overstated by $160

B   understated by $40   **D**   understated by $160

16 On 1 January 20–8, Faisal had a provision for doubtful debts of $3 200. During the year, he wrote off debts of $2 000 as irrecoverable. On 31 December, he adjusted the provision for doubtful debts to $2 800.

What was the net effect on the profit for the year?

A   decrease $1 600   **C**   decrease $4 000

B   decrease $2 400   **D**   decrease $4 800

17 At the end of her financial year on 30 September, Mariam's credit customers owe $15 900. This includes $500 owed by Waseem, which Mariam is not sure she will receive.

Which entries should Mariam make on 30 September?

	Debit	$	Credit	$
A	income statement	500	irrecoverable debts	500
B	income statement	500	provision for doubtful debts	500
C	irrecoverable debts	500	Waseem	500
D	provision for doubtful debts	500	Waseem	500

18 What happens to the total of the irrecoverable debts account at the end of the financial year?

A   It is deducted from the provision for doubtful debts account

B   It is deducted from the trade receivables in the statement of financial position

C   It is transferred to the profit and loss section of the income statement

D   It is transferred to the trading section of the income statement.

Structured questions

1 The following accounts appeared in the ledger of Jane on 31 December 20–7:

Sales account

Date	Details	Folio	$	Date	Details	Folio	$
				20–7			
				Dec 31	Total for year		89 000

Wages and salaries account

Date	Details	Folio	$	Date	Details	Folio	$
20–7							
Dec 31	Total paid		20 500				

Rent receivable account

Date	Details	Folio	$	Date	Details	Folio	$
				20–7			
				Dec 31	Total received		5 200

Purchases returns account

Date	Details	Folio	$	Date	Details	Folio	$
				20–7			
				Dec 31	Total for year		490

Inventory account

Date	Details	Folio	$	Date	Details	Folio	$
20–7							
Jan 1	Balance	b/d	4 400				

Drawings account

Date	Details	Folio	$	Date	Details	Folio	$
20–7							
Dec 31	Total for year		8 000				

Capital account

Date	Details	Folio	$	Date	Details	Folio	$
				20–7			
				Jan 1	Balance	b/d	40 000

a Close the above accounts at 31 December 20–7, as appropriate. The inventory on 31 December 20–7 was valued at $5 300. The profit for the year ended 31 December 20–7 was $6 000.

b Explain why the balance of Jane's capital account has decreased despite the business making a profit. Suggest how Jane could have avoided this.

> **TIP**
>
> Part **a** of this question requires the skill of knowledge and understanding. You need to know the double entry system and understand how it is applied to year-end transfers.
>
> Part **b** of this question requires the skill of analysis. You need to analyse the reason for the change in the balance and how this could be avoided.

2 Mustafa is a financial advisor. He provided the following information for the year ended 30 June 20–4:

	$
Commission receivable	84 000
Interest receivable	2 300
Rent and rates	12 000
Office expenses	8 050
Salary of assistant	25 000
Postages and telephone expenses	4 950

a Prepare Mustafa's income statement for the year ended 30 June 20–4.

b State the difference between gross profit and profit for the year.

c State why it was not possible to calculate a gross profit for Mustafa.

> **TIP**
>
> This question requires the skill of knowledge and understanding. You need to know the principles of preparing an income statement and you need to understand the difference between a trading business and a service business.

3 Haleema is a trader. She provided the following information for the year ended 31 August 20–3:

	$
Revenue	80 000
Purchases	35 000
Sales returns	2 000
Carriage inwards	7 500
Carriage outwards	5 000
Inventory 1 September 20–2	10 000
Inventory 31 August 20–3	16 000
Discount allowed	450
Discount received	230
Operating expenses	18 000
Wages	24 000

a Prepare Haleema's income statement for the year ended 31 August 20–3.

b Complete the table by stating where the debit and credit entry will be for each of the following items when transferring them to the income statement for the year ended 31 August 20–3:

	Debit	Credit
Purchases		
Sales returns		
Operating expenses		
Discount received		
Inventory on1 September 20–2		

4 Kelly is a trader. Her financial year ends on 31 March. The balances remaining on her books at 31 March 20–7 after calculating the gross profit for the year included the following:

	$
Capital 1 April 20–6	50 000
Drawings	2 340
Gross profit	39 100
Wages	18 650
Office expenses	4 470
Motor expenses	1 570
Loan interest paid	250
Discount allowed	950
Rent and rates	9 600
Insurance	2 400
Carriage outwards	1 160
Advertising costs	3 110
Rent receivable	3 000

a Prepare the profit and loss section of the income statement for the year ended 31 March 20–7.

b Write up Kelly's capital account for the year ended 31 March 20–7. Balance the account and bring down the balance.

5 Lee provided the below list of his assets and liabilities.

a Indicate with a tick (✓) the section of Lee's statement of financial position where **each** item would appear.

	Non-current assets	Current assets	Current liabilities	Non-current liabilities	Capital
Machinery					
Inventory					
Trade payables					
Trade receivables					
Drawings					
Petty cash					
Bank overdraft					
Five-year bank loan					
Loss for the year					

b State the order in which non-current assets are usually shown in a statement of financial position. Use an example to illustrate your answer.

c State the order in which current assets are usually shown in a statement of financial position. Use an example to illustrate your answer.

d Explain the meaning of the term 'non-current liabilities'.

6 The following balances remain on the books of Samira on 31 March 20–1 after the preparation of her income statement for the year ended 31 March 20–1:

	$
Capital 1 April 20–0	140 000
Premises	80 000
Inventory 31 March 20–1	12 000
Trade receivables	9 000
Trade payables	12 000
Fixtures and equipment	30 000
Drawings	9 000
Bank overdraft	4 700
Cash	200
Loan from AB Loans (repayable 1 January 20–6)	10 000
Motor vehicles	15 000
Loss for the year	11 500

Prepare Samira's statement of financial position at 31 March 20–1.

75

> **TIP**
> This question requires the skill of knowledge and understanding. You need to know the principles of preparing a statement of financial position and you need to understand how to relate these to the given scenario.

7 Vijay is an IT consultant. His trial balance on 31 May 20–6 was as follows:

Debit	$	Credit	$
Premises	50 000	Capital 1 June 20–5	80 000
Trade receivables	12 500	Trade payables	1 600
Office equipment	10 400	Fees from clients	136 000
Salaries	72 500	Rent receivable	10 000
Motor vehicles	9 300		
Motor vehicle expenses	1 480		
Bank	13 900		
Discount allowed	2 100		
Petty cash	100		
Office expenses	13 570		
Rates and insurance	6 750		
Drawings	35 000		
	227 600		227 600

Prepare Vijay's income statement for the year ended 31 May 20–6 and a statement of financial position at 31 May 20–6.

8   Bethany's trial balance at 31 July 20–9 was as follows:

	Debit $	Credit $
Capital 1 August 20–8		70 000
Drawings	4 100	
Premises	50 000	
Fixtures and fittings	10 600	
Office equipment	4 900	
Bank charges	300	
Lighting and heating	2 500	
Rates and insurance	5 100	
Repairs and maintenance	3 080	
Operating expenses	2 070	
Carriage inwards	7 500	
Carriage outwards	2 950	
Commission receivable		4 000
Revenue		62 000
Purchases	36 000	
Sales returns	2 000	
Purchases returns		3 000
Inventory 1 June 20–8	7 000	
Bank	1 330	
Trade receivables	2 230	
Trade payables		2 660
	141 660	141 660

Inventory on 31 July 20–9 was valued at $6 100.

a   Prepare Bethany's income statement for the year ended 31 July 20–9 and a statement of financial position at 31 July 20–9.

Bethany is considering whether or not to extend her premises. The cost would be $30 000. This would improve her working conditions but would not affect the operating profit.

b   Advise Bethany on whether or not she should proceed with this plan.

TIP

Part **a** of this question requires the skill of knowledge and understanding. You need to know the principles of preparing financial statements and understand how to relate these to the given scenario.

Part **b** requires the skill of evaluation. You need to evaluate the information provided and draw a reasoned conclusion.

9   Emily has recently opened a business but does not understand some of the accounting terms
    and principles.

   a   Explain what is meant by **each** of the following accounting principles. Use examples to
    illustrate your answer.

      i   business entity

      ii   going concern

      iii   duality

      iv   historic cost.

   b   'It is important that financial statements can be understood by the users of those statements'.
    State the accounting object being described.

   c   Explain the accounting term 'comparability'.

   d   The information provided in financial statements can be regarded as reliable if it is capable of
    being independently verified.

     State **two** other conditions which must be present for such information to be reliable.

TIP
This question requires the skill of knowledge and understanding. You need to know the accounting
principles and objectives. You need to demonstrate your understanding by providing examples of
how the principles are applied.

10 a   State **two** features of each of the following:

      i   capital expenditure

      ii   revenue expenditure

      iii   capital receipts

      iv   revenue receipts.

   b   State whether **each** of the following payments represents capital expenditure or revenue
    expenditure:

      i   purchase price of premises

      ii   legal fees for the purchase of premises

      iii   insurance of premises

      iv   repainting outside of premises

      v   installation of air conditioning in premises.

   c   Explain the effect on the profit for the year if $100 for the payment of motor vehicle expenses
    was included in the motor vehicles account.

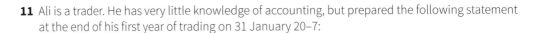

11 Ali is a trader. He has very little knowledge of accounting, but prepared the following statement at the end of his first year of trading on 31 January 20–7:

	$	$
Sale of goods	36 000	
Proceeds of sale of $\frac{1}{4}$ of equipment	1 000	37 000
Less Purchases of goods	18 000	
Purchases of equipment	4 000	
	22 000	
Less Closing inventory of goods	1 500	
	20 500	
General expenses	5 220	
Rent and rates	8 100	
Insurance	450	
Drawings from bank	10 000	44 270
Loss		7 270

a Redraft the above statement, using a correct heading and correct format.

b Select **two** of the items you have not included in your statement and explain why you have **not** included these items.

c Explain how the value of the non-current assets would be affected by the errors Ali made when preparing his income statement.

12 Martha started a business trading in wooden toys on 1 July 20–5. At the end of the first year of trading, she valued her inventory at the lower of cost and net realisable value.

a Explain the meaning of the term 'cost'.

b Explain the meaning of the term 'net realisable value'.

c Explain how Martha is applying the accounting principle of prudence by valuing her inventory at the lower of cost and net realisable value.

Martha provided the following information about her inventory on 30 June 20–6 at the end of her first year of trading:

Code number	Number of units	Cost price per unit $	Selling price per unit $
DZ22	410	21	18
LS15	290	15	22
SH49	300	25	36

The cost per unit of LS15 does not include carriage inwards of $2 per unit.

d Calculate the value of **each** type of inventory. Show your calculations.

e Explain the basis for your valuation in each case.

After Martha had prepared her financial statements for her second year of trading, it was discovered that she had overvalued her closing inventory by $500.

f Complete the table to show the effect of this error by placing a tick (✔) in the correct columns:

	Overstated	Understated	No effect
Profit for the year ended 30 June 20–7			
Current assets at 30 June 20–7			
Martha's capital at 1 July 20–7			
Gross profit for the year ending 30 June 20–8			
Current assets at 30 June 20–8			

> **TIP**
>
> Parts **a–e** of this question require the skill of knowledge and understanding. You need to know the principles of inventory valuation and understand how this is applied to a given scenario.
>
> Part **f** requires the skill of analysis. You need to analyse the effect of the error.

13 Yee's payments for the year ended 31 December 20–8 included the following:

	$
Wages	68 000
Insurance (for 12 months to 30 June 20–9)	2 400

At 1 January 20–8, wages due amounted to $1 300 and insurance prepaid amounted to $1 140. At 31 December 20–8, wages due amounted to $1 550.

Write up the wages account and the insurance account as they would appear in Yee's ledger for the year ended 31 December 20–8. Balance the accounts and show the amounts transferred to the income statement.

14 Zeema's financial year ends on 30 September. She sublets part of her premises to Faith at an annual rent of $6 600.

On 1 October 20–3, Faith owed one month's rent. During the year ended 30 September 20–4, Faith paid rent of $8 250.

a Write up Zeema's rent receivable account for the year ended 30 September 20–4. Balance the account and show the amount transferred to the income statement.

b Prepare a relevant extract from Zeema's income statement for the year ended 30 September 20–4.

15 Mandeep's financial year ends on 30 June.

On 1 January 20–4, Mandeep sublet part of his premises to Mahender at an annual rent of $2 600, payable quarterly in advance. Mandeep received bank transfers from Mahender representing three month's rent on 1 January, 1 April and 30 June 20–4.

a Write up the rent receivable account as it would appear in Mandeep's ledger for the year ended 30 June 20–4. Balance the account and show the amount transferred to the income statement.

Aneela pays Mandeep a commission on any goods purchased from her by Mandeep's customers. The commission is paid quarterly in arrears. During Mandeep's financial year ended 30 June 20–4, he received bank transfers for commission as follows:

	$
2 July 20–3	520
3 October 20–3	410
3 January 20–4	630
2 March 20–4	340

On 1 July 20–3, $520 commission was outstanding, and on 30 June 20–4, $480 commission was outstanding.

b Write up the commission receivable account as it would appear in Mandeep's ledger for the year ended 30 June 20–4. Balance the account and show the amount transferred to the income statement.

c State and explain the accounting principle which Mandeep is applying in his treatment of rent receivable and commission receivable.

TIP

This question requires the skill of knowledge and understanding. You need to know how to record income receivable and the treatment of accrued income. You need to demonstrate your understanding by making the entries in the ledger and explaining the accounting principle that is applied.

16 Jenny is a trader. Her trial balance at 31 December 20–6 was as follows:

Debit	$	Credit	$
Drawings	17 000	Capital 1 January 20–6	110 000
Premises	80 000	Revenue	350 000
Fixtures and fittings	14 000	Purchases returns	10 000
Motor vehicles	9 500	Discount received	4 100
Purchases	280 000	Rent receivable	5 500
Inventory 1 January 20–6	20 000	Trade payables	23 300
Carriage inwards	5 000	Bank overdraft	17 200
Operating expenses	12 200		
Rates and insurance	5 490		
Repairs and maintenance	3 870		
Salaries	41 000		
Motor vehicle expenses	2 940		
Trade receivables	29 100		
	520 100		520 100

The following additional information is available:

1   Inventory at 31 December 20–6 was valued at $24 000.

2   At 31 December 20–6 rent receivable due amounted to $500 and salaries due amounted to $3 500.

3   Insurance, $2 800, paid during the year was for 14 months to 28 February 20–6.

4   Bank charges amounting to $790 had not been entered in the books.

a   Prepare Jenny's income statement for the year ended 31 December 20–6 and a statement of financial position at that date.

Jenny's bank has proposed that the bank overdraft should be converted to a three-year bank loan. Annual interest would have to be paid but this would be at a lower percentage than that charged on the overdraft. The loan would be repayable in full at the end of the three-year period.

b   Advise Jenny on whether or not to agree to the bank's proposal.

TIP

Part **a** of this question requires the skill of knowledge and understanding. You need to know the principles of preparing financial statements and understand how to relate these to the given scenario.

Part **b** requires the skill of evaluation. You need to evaluate the information provided and draw a reasoned conclusion.

17 The following balance remained on the books of Leo after the calculation of his gross profit for the year ended 31 October 20–7:

	$	$
Gross profit		34 500
Equipment	32 000	
Fixtures and fittings	13 600	
Capital 1 November 20–6		44 000
Drawings	5 000	
Stationery	380	
Wages	19 800	
Inventory 31 October 20–7	6 500	
Trade receivables	3 740	
Trade payables		3 500
Rent and rates	2 600	
Office expenses	3 100	
Heating and lighting	2 200	
Bank overdraft		2 120
Bank charges	200	
Five-year loan from FS Limited		5 000
	89 120	89 120

The following additional information is available:

1 At 31 October 20–7: rates prepaid amounted to $220

wages outstanding amounted to $790

inventory of stationery was valued at $95.

2 Leo borrowed $5 000 from FS Limited on 1 November 20–6. Interest is charged at the rate of 5% per annum.

a Prepare Leo's income statement for the year ended 31 October 20–7.

b Prepare Leo's statement of financial position at 31 October 20–7.

18 Omar started business on 1 August 20–1. On that date, he purchased machinery costing $20 000. He estimated that the machinery would last for five years, when it would have a residual value of $2 000. At the end of his financial year, Omar was advised to depreciate his machinery.

a Explain what is meant by depreciation.

b State **two** causes of depreciation.

c State **two** reasons why it is necessary to charge depreciation.

d Name **two** accounting principles which are observed by charging depreciation.

e Calculate the depreciation charge for **each** of the three years ended 31 July 20–2, 20–3 and 20–4 using:

i the straight line method of depreciation

ii the reducing balance method of depreciation at 40% per annum.

19 Gugu began business on 1 May 20–1. On that date, she purchased equipment, $30 000, on credit from Superquip. She decided to use the straight line method of depreciation at the rate of 20% per annum, calculated from the date of purchase.

On 1 November 20–2, Gugu purchased additional equipment, $10 000, and paid by bank transfer.

a Write up the equipment account and the provision for depreciation of equipment account in Gugu's ledger for the two years ended 30 April 20–2 and 30 April 20–3.

b Prepare a relevant extract from Gugu's income statement for the year ended 30 April 20–3.

c Prepare a relevant extract from Gugu's statement of financial position at 30 April 20–3.

During the financial year ended 30 April 20–4, no equipment was purchased or sold. When calculating the depreciation of equipment for the year ended 30 April 20–4, the reducing balance method was applied instead of the straight line method.

d Explain the effect of this error on the profit for the year and the value of equipment appearing in the statement of financial position.

TIP

Parts **a–c** of this question require the skill of knowledge and understanding. You need to know the principles of depreciation. You need to demonstrate your understanding by relating the principles to the given scenario.

Part **d** of this question requires the skill of analysis. You need to analyse the effect of the error.

20 Dinesh started business on 1 January 20–3 on which date he bought two machines costing $9 000 each, paying by bank transfer. He decided to depreciate the machines using the straight line method at 20% per annum, calculated on the cost of machines held at the end of each financial year.

On 30 June 20–6 Dinesh sold one machine for $2 800 which he received in cash.

On 1 July 20–6 Dinesh purchased a new machine, $12 000, on credit from Western Ltd.

  a **i** Calculate the cost of machinery held on 1 January 20–6. Enter this as a balance in the machinery account.

      ii Calculate the total depreciation up to 1 January 20–6. Enter this as a balance in the provision for depreciation of machinery account.

  b Make the necessary entries in the nominal ledger accounts of Dinesh for the year ended 31 December 20–6. Balance the accounts as necessary.

21 a Explain how depreciation is an example of the application of the principle of matching **and** the principle of prudence.

   b Explain why it is important that the same method of depreciation is used each year for the same type of asset.

Melody started business on 1 October 20–4. On that date, she purchased equipment, $10 000, on credit from Superquip. Melody decided to depreciate equipment using the straight line method at 20% per annum calculated on the cost of assets held at the end of each financial year.

On 1 October 20–5 Melody purchased additional equipment, $4 000, paying by cheque. On 31 March 20–7, Melody sold half of the original equipment (purchased on 1 October 20–4) for $1 800, cash.

   c Write up the equipment account, provision for depreciation of equipment account and equipment disposal account for the three years ended 30 September 20–5, 20–6 and 20–7.

   d Prepare a relevant extract from Melody's income statement for the year ended 30 September 20–7.

   e Prepare a relevant extract from Melody's statement of financial position at 30 September 20–7.

22 Dave is a business consultant. His trial balance at 31 July 20–9 was as follows:

	$	$
Capital 1 August 20–8		68 000
Drawings	18 600	
Premises at cost	55 000	
Fixtures and fittings at cost	9 500	
Motor vehicles at cost	28 000	
Provision for depreciation of fixtures and fittings		950
Provision for depreciation of motor vehicles		5 600
Long term loan from QT Limited		10 000
Fees		102 000
Office expenses	11 550	
Rates and insurance	11 400	
Wages and salaries	42 500	
Motor expenses	3 650	
Loan interest	300	
Trade receivables	7 800	
Trade payables		590
Bank overdraft		1 160
	188 300	188 300

Dave provided the following additional information:

1   At 31 July 20–9 rates and insurance prepaid amounted to $320.

2   A bank statement received on 31 July 20–9 showed bank charges, $140. This had not been recorded in the accounting records.

3   The loan from QT Limited was received on 1 August 20–8. Interest is charged at the rate of 6% per annum.

4   Depreciation is charged on the fixtures and fittings at 10% per annum using the straight line method and at 20% per annum on the motor vehicles using the reducing balance method.

a   Prepare Dave's income statement for the year ended 31 July 20–9.

b   Prepare Dave's statement of financial position at 31 July 20–9.

23 Varsha is a trader. She provided the following trial balance at 31 December 20–0:

	$	$
Purchases	120 000	
Revenue		190 000
Inventory 1 January 20–0	7 000	
Premises at cost	40 000	
Equipment at cost	19 000	
Provision for depreciation of equipment		5 700
Motor vehicles	12 000	
Provision for depreciation of motor vehicles		4 320
Operating expenses	21 200	
Wages	31 750	
Rates and insurance	9 200	
Loan interest paid	90	
Commission receivable		4 000
Discount received		1 950
Trade receivables	14 400	
Trade payables		8 940
Bank	5 790	
Capital 1 January 20–0		68 000
Drawings	8 480	
Long term loan – A1 Finance		6 000
	288 910	288 910

Varsha supplied the following additional information:

1   Inventory at 31 December 20–0 was valued at $8 500.

2   At 31 December 20–0, commission receivable due amounted to $200 and wages due amounted to $2 140.

3   The amount paid for rates, $4 800, is for 15 months to 31 March 20–1.

4   During the year ended 31 December 20–0 Varsha took goods costing $940 for her own use. This has not been entered in the accounting records.

5   The loan from A1 Finance was obtained on 1 July 20–0 and interest is charged at 6% per annum.

6   Depreciation on equipment is charged at 10% per annum using the straight line method and depreciation on motor vehicles is charged at 20% per annum using the reducing balance method.

a   Prepare the income statement of Varsha for the year ended 31 December 20–0.

b   Prepare the statement of financial position of Varsha at 31 December 20–0.

> **TIP**
> This question requires the skill of knowledge and understanding. You need to know the principles of preparing financial statements and understand how to relate these to the given scenario.

24 Waqas is a trader selling on credit terms. His financial year ends on 31 August. During the year ended 31 August 20–2, some debts were irrecoverable. At the end of the financial year, he decided to create a provision for doubtful debts.

    a Explain the meaning of the terms:

        i irrecoverable debts

        ii debts written off recovered

        iii provision for doubtful debts.

    Waqas decided that the provision created on 31 August 20–2 should be 3% of the trade receivables and that it should be maintained at the same percentage of trade receivables at the end of each financial year. He provided the following information:

	$
31 August 20–2 Total trade receivables	5 500
31 August 20–3 Total trade receivables	6 200
31 August 20–4 Total trade receivables	4 900

    b Write up the provision for doubtful debts account as it would appear in the ledger of Waqas for the three years ended 31 August 20–2, 31 August 20–3 and 31 August 20–4.

    c Prepare a relevant extract from the statement of financial position of Waqas at 31 August 20–2, 31 August 20–3 and 31 August 20–4.

25 Hiba's financial year ends on 31 October. Hiba's trade receivables amounted to $34 250 on 28 October 20–7. This included the following amounts which had been outstanding for over two years:

	$
J Mavuso	480
K Ngwenga	1 520
L Makamba	250

On 30 October 20–7:

1 Hiba decided to write off L Makamba's debt as irrecoverable.

2 J Mavuso sent a cheque for $450 and a letter to say that he was unable to pay the balance. Hiba wrote off the balance as irrecoverable.

3 A letter was received stating that K Ngwenga was bankrupt. A cheque was enclosed for a first and final dividend of 70c in the $. Hiba wrote off the remaining balance as irrecoverable.

On 31 October 20–7, Hiba decided to create a provision for doubtful debts of $2\frac{1}{2}$% of the remaining trade receivables.

    a Write up the following accounts in Hiba's ledger:

        • J Mavuso account

        • K Ngwenga account

        • L Makamba account

        • Irrecoverable debts account

        • Provision for doubtful debts account.

Hiba's trade receivables on 31 October 20–8 were $1 000 lower than they were on 31 October 20–7. Hiba decided to discontinue the provision for doubtful debts.

b Discuss the effects of this decision.

> **TIP**
>
> Part **a** of this question requires the skill of knowledge and understanding. You need to know the principles of recording irrecoverable debts and provisions for doubtful debts and you need to understand how to apply them in the given scenario.
>
> Part **b** of this question requires the skill of analysis. You need to analyse the effects of the owner's decision.

26 The following accounts appeared in the ledger of Sanath whose financial year ends on 30 June:

				Irrecoverable debts account				
Date	Details	Folio	$	Date	Details	Folio	$
20–4				20–5			
Oct 1	PK Stores		200	Jun 30	Income statement		450
20–5							
May 1	Sellfast & Co		250				
			450				450

				Provision for doubtful debts account				
Date	Details	Folio	$	Date	Details	Folio	$
20–5				20–4			
June 30	Income statement		100	July 1	Balance	b/d	700
	Balance	c/d	600				
			700				700
				20–5			
				July 1	Balance	b/d	600

Explain **each** entry in the above accounts and also state where the double entry for **each** entry will be found.

> **TIP**
>
> This question requires the skill of knowledge and understanding. You need to know the entries required to complete accounts for irrecoverable debts and the provision for doubtful debts. You need to understand how to relate these entries to the accounts provided.

87

27 Alice's financial year ends on 30 November. On 1 December 20–3, the balance on her provision for doubtful debts account was $500. On 1 November 20–4, Alice's debtors included Safat Stores who owed $590 and El Nil Traders who owed $1 400.

Alice's transactions for the month ended 30 November 20–4 included the following:

November 5   Received a cheque from El Nil Traders in settlement of their account less a 2% cash discount.

          14   Sold goods, $420, on credit to El Nil Traders.

          25   Received a cheque for $50 from Ramsis Road Traders whose account had been written off as irrecoverable in June 20–2.

          27   Received a cheque, $490, for a final settlement of the amount owed by Safat Stores who were bankrupt. Alice wrote off the remaining balance as irrecoverable.

          30   Decided to maintain her provision for doubtful debts at 4% of the trade receivables, who owed $13 500 on that date.

a   Write up the following accounts in Alice's ledger:

- Safat Stores account
- El Nil Traders account
- Irrecoverable debts account
- Debts recovered account
- Provision for doubtful debts account.

b   Prepare a relevant extract from Alice's income statement for the year ended 30 November 20–4.

c   Prepare a relevant extract from Alice's statement of financial position at 30 November 20–4.

d   State and explain **one** accounting principle that Alice is applying by maintaining a provision for doubtful debts.

28 Thabo owns a gardening and home services business. He provided the following trial balance on 28 February 20–7:

Debit	$	Credit	$
Drawings	9 200	Capital 1 March 20–6	30 000
Bank	1 040	Trade payables	750
Trade receivables	4 300	Provision for doubtful debts	200
Equipment at valuation	10 860	Income from customers	42 000
Motor vehicles at valuation	16 000	Commission receivable	2 420
Motor expenses	2 850		
Insurance	1 970		
Repairs & maintenance	2 590		
Wages	26 100		
Irrecoverable debts	150		
Operating expenses	310		
	75 370		75 370

The following additional information is available:

1 Operating expenses owing 28 February 20–7 amounted to $43.

2 Motor expenses includes motor insurance, $806, for 13 months to 31 March 20–7.

3 The provision for doubtful debts is maintained at 5% of the trade receivables at the end of each financial year.

4 The non-current assets are depreciated using the revaluation method. On 28 February 20–7, the equipment was valued at $10 120 and the motor vehicles were valued at $13 850.

Prepare Thabo's income statement for the year ended 28 February 20–7 and a statement of financial position at 28 February 20–7.

29 Kala is a trader. The following is her trial balance at 31 May 20–9 after the calculation of the gross profit:

Debit	$	Credit	$
Rent	13 100	Gross profit	140 000
Rates and insurance	8 100	Discount received	3 200
Wages	79 500	Provision for depreciation	
Office expenses	2 100	of fixtures and fittings	7 410
Operating expenses	6 300	Provision for depreciation	
Fixtures and fittings at cost	39 000	of motor vehicles	6 480
Motor vehicles at cost	18 000	Trade payables	31 500
Inventory 31 May 20–9	39 050	Provision for doubtful debts	850
Trade receivables	24 300	Capital 1 June 20–8	70 000
Bank	12 190		
Drawings	17 800		
	259 440		259 440

Kala provided the following additional information:

1 The operating expenses include telephone expenses. At 31 May 20–9, a telephone account of $80 was unpaid.

2 The office expenses include office stationery. At 31 May 20–9, there was an inventory of stationery valued at $122.

3 $100 owing by a credit customer should be written off as irrecoverable.

4 The provision for doubtful debts should be adjusted to equal 3% of the remaining trade receivables.

5 The non-current assets are depreciated using the reducing balance method at the rate of 10% per annum for the fixtures and fittings and 20% per annum for the motor vehicles.

a Prepare Kala's income statement (profit and loss section) for the year ended 31 May 20–9.

b Prepare Kala's statement of financial position at 31 May 20–9.

30 Tahir is a trader. His financial year ends on 31 May. After the preparation of the trading account section of the income statement for the year ended 31 May 20–4, the following balances remained on his books:

	$
Gross profit	42 000
Premises at cost	60 000
Fixtures and equipment at cost	22 000
Motor vehicles at cost	18 000
Trade receivables	9 900
Trade payables	7 480
Administration expenses	4 950
Motor expenses	3 260
Provision for doubtful debts	420
Irrecoverable debts	270
Commission receivable	2 800
6% loan (repayable in 15 years)	10 000
Loan interest paid	300
Wages	22 400
Rates and insurance	4 300
Provision for depreciation of fixtures and equipment	6 600
Provision for depreciation of motor vehicles	6 480
Inventory 31 May 20–4	8 200
Capital 1 June 20–3	86 500
Drawings	5 500
Bank	3 200 Dr

The following additional information is available:

1 At 31 May 20–4:

Commission receivable outstanding amounted to $160.

Six months loan interest is outstanding.

The rates and insurance amount of $4 300 includes $1 800 insurance, which represents 18 months' insurance to 30 November 20–4.

2 The provision for doubtful debts is to be maintained at 4% of the trade receivables.

3 The fixtures and equipment are being depreciated at 15% per annum using the straight line method.

4 The motor vehicles are being depreciated at 20% per annum using the reducing balance method.

a Prepare the income statement of Tahir for the year ended 31 May 20–4.

b Prepare the statement of financial position of Tahir at 31 May 20–4.

Section 4 (*Chapters 14–22 of the Coursebook*)

Multiple choice questions

1 After Suzanne received her bank statement, she updated her cash book and prepared a bank reconciliation statement.

Which item did Suzanne include in her bank reconciliation statement?

A bank charges	**C** dishonoured cheque
B direct debit	**D** unpresented cheque.

2 After receiving his bank statement, Idris updated his cash book.

Which item on his bank statement would Idris debit in his cash book?

A bank interest on deposit account	**C** customer's cheque dishonoured
B credit transfer to a supplier	**D** direct debit for rent.

3 Jonny's bank statement showed a balance $500 greater than the balance in the bank column of his cash book.

What could have caused this?

A a cheque not yet credited by the bank

B a cheque not yet presented to the bank

C a direct debit for insurance not yet entered in the cash book

D interest on a bank loan not yet entered in the cash book.

4 A cheque received from Abdul for $420 was incorrectly debited to Abdiel's account.

Which journal entry corrects this error?

		Debit $	Credit $
A	Abdiel	420	
	Abdul		420
B	Abdiel	420	
	Abdul	420	
	Suspense		840
C	Abdul	420	
	Abdiel		420
D	Suspense	840	
	Abdiel		420
	Abdul		420

5 Ellie's fixtures originally cost $15 000. The current book value is $9 600. Depreciation is calculated using the reducing balance method at 20% per annum.

Which journal entry will Ellie make at the end of her financial year on 31 May 20–3?

		Debit $	Credit $
A	Income statement	1 080	
	Provision for depreciation of fixtures		1 080
B	Income statement	1 920	
	Provision for depreciation of fixtures		1 920
C	Provision for depreciation of fixtures	1 080	
	Income statement		1 080
D	Provision for depreciation of fixtures	1 920	
	Income statement		1 920

6 Leroy is a trader. He made the following journal entry:

	Debit $	Credit $
Discount allowed	200	
Discount received	200	
Suspense		400
Correction of error		

What error is being corrected?

A Discount allowed, $200, was incorrectly credited to discount received account.

B Discount allowed, $200, was incorrectly debited to discount received account.

C Discount received, $200, was incorrectly credited to discount allowed account.

D Discount received, $200, was incorrectly debited to discount allowed account.

7 Loliwe provided the following information:

		$
May 1	Debit balance on sales ledger control account	4 650
31	Payments to credit suppliers	4 015
	Receipts from credit customers	3 900
	Discount received	135
	Discount allowed	100
	Cash sales	1 974
	Credit sales	5 017

What was the debit balance on the sales ledger control account on 1 June?

A $5 517   **B** $5 667   **C** $7 491   **D** $7 641

8 Which item is credited to a purchases ledger control account?

    A discount received   **C** purchases returns

    B interest on overdue account   **D** transfer to sales ledger

9 Bheki is both a supplier and a customer of Robert. Bheki's account in Robert's sales ledger showed a debit balance of $55 and his account in Robert's purchases ledger showed a credit balance of $190.

Which journal entry would Robert make to set the balance on the sales ledger account against the balance on the purchases ledger account?

		Debit $	Credit $
A	Bheki account in purchases ledger	55	
	Bheki account in sales ledger		55
B	Bheki account in purchases ledger	135	
	Bheki account in sales ledger		135
C	Bheki account in sales ledger	55	
	Bheki account in purchases ledger		55
D	Bheki account in sales ledger	135	
	Bheki account in purchases ledger		135

10 Karim provided the following information:

	$
Revenue	80 000
Cost of sales	62 500
Opening inventory	21 600
Closing inventory	22 200

What was the rate of inventory turnover?

    A 1.43 times   **B** 1.83 times   **C** 2.85 times   **D** 3.65 times

11 A trader does not maintain a full set of accounting records.

How may his profit for the year be calculated?

    A Closing capital – Drawings – Opening capital

    B Closing capital – Drawings + Capital introduced – Opening capital

    C Closing capital + Capital introduced – Opening capital

    D Closing capital + Drawings – Capital introduced – Opening capital

12 Cindy provided the following information:

	$	$
Revenue		43 400
Opening inventory	3 400	
Purchases	36 500	
	39 900	
Closing inventory	3 500	36 400
Gross profit		7 000

What was Cindy's gross profit margin?

A 16.13% **B** 17.54% **C** 19.18% **D** 19.23%

13 On 1 March 20–8, a cricket club purchased a minibus for taking teams to away matches and made the following payments on that date:

	$
Cost of minibus	18 500
Fuel for minibus	120
Insurance for minibus for 24 months	960

What will appear in the receipts and payments account and the income and expenditure account for the year ended 28 February 20–9:

	Receipts and payments account $	Income and expenditure account $
A	18 500	1 080
B	19 100	600
C	19 580	600
D	19 580	1 080

14 The debit side of a receipts and payments account totalled $4 870 and the credit side totalled $5 670.

What does the difference between these totals represent?

A bank overdraft **C** deficit for the year
B cash at bank **D** surplus for the year

15 The financial year of a sports club ends on 30 June. The club rents a training ground at an annual rent of $2 400. On 1 July 20–4, the club owed two months' rent. During the year ended 30 June 20–5, a total of $3 000 was paid for rent.

How much was recorded for rent in the receipts and payments account for the year ended 30 June 20–5?

A $2 000 **B** $2 400 **C** $2 800 **D** $3 000

16 Which items are credited to a partner's current account?

1 interest on capital

2 interest on drawings

3 interest on loan from partner

4 share of loss for the year

A 1 and 2   **B** 1 and 3   **C** 2 and 4   **D** 3 and 4

17 Heng and Magda are in partnership. They provided the following information:

	$	$
Gross profit for the year		78 650
Administration expenses		14 330
Salaries – Employees	35 200	
Magda	10 000	45 200
Interest on loan – From bank	500	
From Heng	220	720

What was the profit for the year?

A $18 400   **B** $18 620   **C** $28 400   **D** $28 620

18 Farid and Kadar are in partnership. Farid had a debit balance of $240 on his current account.

What does this mean?

A He had a bank overdraft of $240.

B He had $240 in the bank.

C He owed the business $240.

D He was owed $240 by the business.

19 A manufacturer provided the following information at the end of his financial year:

	$
Cost of raw material consumed	44 500
Wages – Factory production workers	37 650
Factory supervisors	12 460
Office workers	21 330
Overheads – Factory	20 950
Office	11 820

What was the cost of production?

A $82 150   **B** $94 610   **C** $115 560   **D** $148 710

20 Why is a manufacturing account prepared?

A to calculate cost of goods produced

B to calculate cost of materials consumed

C to calculate factory overheads

D to calculate prime cost.

21 A manufacturer overvalued his closing inventory of work in progress at the end of his financial year on 31 December 20–6.

What was the effect on the financial statements for the year ended 31 December 20–7?

	Cost of production		Gross profit			Current assets		
	Over-stated	Under-stated	Over-stated	Under-stated	No effect	Over-stated	Under-stated	No effect
A	✓		✓			✓		
B	✓			✓				✓
C		✓		✓				✓
D		✓			✓		✓	

22 The financial year of XX Limited ends on 31 August. Debentures were issued on 1 January 20–4. Interest was to be paid annually in arrears on 31 December.

Where would debenture interest appear in the financial statements for the year ended 31 August 20–4?

	Income statement	Statement of changes in equity	Statement of financial position
A	✓		
B	✓		✓
C		✓	
D		✓	✓

23 Which statement about holders of preference shares is correct?

A They are entitled to one vote per share.

B They are regarded as members of the company.

C They receive a fixed percentage of the profit.

D They receive a fixed rate of dividend.

24 Which items appear in a statement of changes in equity?

1 interest on debentures paid

2 interim ordinary share dividend paid during the current financial year

3 proposed final ordinary share dividend for the current financial year

4 transfer to general reserve.

A 1 and 2 **B** 1 and 3 **C** 2 and 4 **D** 3 and 4

25 Phewa is a sole trader. Which ratio can she calculate using the information in her statement of financial position?

A gross margin **C** rate of inventory turnover

B profit margin **D** return on capital employed

26 Thembi provided the following information at the end of her financial year:

	$
Non-current assets	290 000
Current assets	34 000
Current liabilities	22 000

Thembi's return on capital employed was 7%.

What was the profit for the year?

A $20 300   **B** $21 140   **C** $22 680   **D** $24 220

27 How can trade payables turnover be calculated?

A $\dfrac{\text{Credit purchases}}{\text{Trade payables}} \times \dfrac{365}{1}$ **C** $\dfrac{\text{Trade payables}}{\text{Credit purchases}} \times \dfrac{365}{1}$

B $\dfrac{\text{Total purchases}}{\text{Trade payables}} \times \dfrac{365}{1}$ **D** $\dfrac{\text{Trade payables}}{\text{Total purchases}} \times \dfrac{365}{1}$

Structured questions

1 The pages of Dwight's cash book relating to June 20–0 were damaged when a bottle of ink was spilt. He obtained a copy of his bank statement which showed a positive bank balance of $3 540 on 30 June.

When comparing his bank statement with his paying-in book and cheque book, Dwight found the following:

1 Cheques sent to the following creditors had not been presented for payment:

	$
Beach Street Stores	295
Jamaica Road Boutique	182
Kingston Kids Ltd	304

2 The following amounts paid into the bank on 29 June had not been credited by the bank:

	$
Cash sales	935
Cheques received from Hi-Fashion Ltd	242
Bermuda Road Boutique	187

Calculate the balance which appeared in the bank column of Dwight's cash book on 30 June 20–0. Show your calculations.

2   Christina balanced her cash book on 31 October 20–4 and brought down a debit balance of $3 280 on 1 November. Her bank statement for October 20–4 showed a closing credit balance of $208.

When comparing the cash book with the bank statement, Christina found the following:

1   These items appeared only in the cash book:

Cheque, $280, paid to Wilma, a creditor supplier

Cash sales $1 643

2   These items appeared only on the bank statement:

Bank charges of $109

Insurance, $850, paid by standing order

3   The bank had debited Christina's business bank account with a standing order for $750, for a life insurance policy premium which should have been paid from Christina's personal bank account.

a   Make any additional entries required in Christina's cash book. Calculate a new bank balance at 31 October 20–4. Bring down the balance on 1 November 20–4.

b   Prepare a bank reconciliation statement at 31 October 20–4.

c   State the bank balance that should be shown in Christina's statement of financial position on 31 October 20–4 and state whether it is an asset or a liability.

3   Wendy is a trader.

a   State **two** reasons why she should reconcile the balance on her bank statement with that shown in her cash book.

b   Explain why items are recorded on the opposite side of a cash book to that on which they appear on a bank statement.

Wendy's cash book (bank columns) showed the following entries for September 20–8.:

Cash book (bank columns only)							
Date	Details	Folio	$	Date	Details	Folio	$
20–8				20–8			
Sept 1	Balance		310	Sept 12	Cheung Ltd		1 750
8	East & West		290	18	W Tong & Co		1 300
14	Chan & Co		1 070				
29	J Tan		95				
30	Cash sales		1 020				
	Balance	c/d	265				
			3 050				3 050
				20–8			
				Oct 1	Balance	b/d	265

The following bank statement was received by Wendy:

	THE NEW BANK LIMITED ANYTOWN			
Customer: Wendy Vine		**Account No:** 679834		
		Date:	30 September 20–8	
Date	**Details**	**Debit** $	**Credit** $	**Balance** $
20–8				
Sept 1	Balance			440 Cr
4	Cheque No. 23457	130		310 Cr
13	Credit No. 3466		290	600 Cr
16	Cheque No. 23458	1 750		1 150 Dr
18	SO Insurance Co	195		1 345 Dr
22	Credit No. 3467		1 070	275 Dr
23	AB Ltd – Dividend received		204	71 Dr
30	Dishonoured cheque	290		361 Dr
	Charges	188		549 Dr

c Explain why the balance on Wendy's cash book on 1 September was not the same as the balance on the bank statement on that date.

d Make any additional entries that are required in the cash book of Wendy. Calculate a new bank balance at 30 September 20–8. Bring down the balance on 1 October 20–8.

e Prepare a bank reconciliation statement at 30 September 20–8.

4 Raminder is a trader. All his sales and purchases are on credit terms, the accounts being settled by cheque. All expenses are paid by cheque.

Raminder's transactions for January 20–7 included the following:

		$
January 4	Cheque received from Aswan	2 400
10	Cheque paid to Ali (Cheque number 12456)	950
17	Cheque paid to Hassan (Cheque number 12457)	3 050
22	Cheque paid for rates (Cheque number 12458)	685
29	Cheque paid for wages (Cheque number 12459)	1 550
30	Cheque received from Ahmed	784

Raminder had a debit balance of $8 280 in his bank column in his cash book on 1 January 20–7.

Raminder received the following bank statement from his bank:

NEW BANK LIMITED ANYTOWN				
Customer: Raminder Singh		**Account No:** 567443		
		Date: 31 January 20–7		
Date	Details	Debit $	Credit $	Balance $
20–7				
January 1	Balance			8 280 Cr
8	Cheque No. 9985		2 400	10 680 Cr
15	Cheque No. 12456	950		9 730 Cr
18	Cheque No. 12457	3 050		6 680 Cr
26	Cheque No. 12458	685		5 995 Cr
30	SO Landlords Ltd (rent)	450		5 545 Cr
31	Bank charges	110		5 435 Cr

a   Write up the bank columns in Raminder's cash book for January 20–7. Make any adjustments that are necessary after receiving the bank statement.

Balance the cash book and bring down the balance on 1 February 20–7.

b   Prepare Raminder's bank reconciliation statement at 31 January 20–7.

c   Explain the meaning of **each** of the following terms used in connection with bank reconciliation.

   i unpresented cheques

   ii amounts not credited.

Raminder has one employee whom he pays by cheque each month. The employee has asked if he could be paid in cash rather than by cheque.

d   Advise Raminder on whether or not he should change the method of payment of wages.

> **!**
>
> **TIP**
>
> Parts **a–c** require the skill of knowledge and understanding. You need to know terms connected with bank reconciliation and the steps to be taken to perform a reconciliation. You need to understand how to apply this knowledge to the given scenario.
>
> Part **d** requires the skill of evaluation. You need to evaluate the advantages and disadvantages of the proposal and draw a reasoned conclusion.

5 a Explain the difference between the following terms:

    i bank statement and bank reconciliation statement

    ii credit transfer and direct debit.

Zodwa is a trader. On 30 June, she compared her cash book with her bank statement. Her cash book showed an overdraft balance of $320.

The following differences between the cash book and the bank statement were discovered:

1   Cheques paid to suppliers not yet presented for payment:

	$
Charlie	428
Fanwell	910

2   Cash sales, $950, not recorded on the bank statement.

3   A debit on the bank statement of $50 which should have been debited to Zodwa's personal bank account.

b Prepare a bank reconciliation statement to show the balance on the bank statement on 30 June.

    Zodwa prepared her statement of financial position on 30 June.

c State:

    i   the amount which would appear for bank

    ii the section in which that amount would appear.

    Give reasons for your answers.

TIP

This question requires the skill of knowledge and understanding. You need to know the terms used in connection with banking and the principles of preparing a bank reconciliation statement. You need to understand how to apply these principles to the given scenario.

6 Ben started a business on 1 May 20–2. He introduced the following into the business:

	$
Premises	85 000
Fixtures and fittings	18 000
Motor vehicles	11 500
Inventory	9 420

He also introduced $5 300 in cash, $5 100 of which was paid into a business bank account. Ben's father also paid $20 000 into the business bank account as a loan to the business.

a Prepare an opening journal entry for Ben on 1 May 20–2. A narrative is required.

b List **three** uses of a journal, excluding opening entries.

c Explain why the journal is not part of the double entry system.

7 Melissa's financial year ends on 30 November.

On 30 November 20–5 Melissa's ledger accounts included the following:

	$
Sales for the year	74 300
Rates, including a prepayment of $40	1 080
Inventory 1 December 20–4	4 650

On 30 November 20–5:

1 Melissa discovered that no entry had been made to record the purchase of equipment, $5 200, on credit from SQ Limited.

2 $56 owing by Roddy, a credit customer, should be written off as irrecoverable.

3 Inventory was valued at $5 110.

4 Equipment should be depreciated by $790.

Prepare journal entries to record the above transactions, including transfers to the income statement. Narratives are required.

8 Sabeena is a trader. Her financial year ends on 31 January.

On 31 January 20–9, the balances in Sabeena's ledger included the following:

	$
Purchases account	33 100
Sales returns account	1 290
Discount received account	870

a Prepare journal entries to transfer these balances to the income statement for the year ended 31 January 20–9. Narratives are **not** required.

On 31 January 20–9, Sabeena's office expenses account had a debit balance of $1 100. This included $1 000 business expenses, of which $90 was prepaid for the following financial year. The remainder was Sabeena's personal expenses.

b Prepare journal entries to make the necessary year-end transfers from the office expenses account. Narratives are **not** required.

On 31 January 20–9, Sabeena sold her motor vehicle on credit to Scrappers for $4 000. The motor vehicle had cost $10 500 and the depreciation to date amounted to $5 124.

c Prepare entries in Sabeena's journal to record the disposal of the motor vehicle. Narratives are **not** required.

On 31 January 20–9, Sabeena's trade receivables amounted to $12 140. Her provision for doubtful debts was $400. The irrecoverable debts written off during the year amounted to $271.

On 31 January 20–9, Sabeena decided to write off $140 owed by Raj (included in the total trade receivables) and to adjust the provision for doubtful debts so that it equalled 4% of the remaining trade receivables.

d Prepare journal entries to record the writing off of the irrecoverable debt, the adjustment of the provision for doubtful debts and year-end transfers to the income statement. Narratives are **not** required.

9 Yee's financial year ends on 31 August. On 31 August 20-0 he opened a suspense account and entered $263 on the credit side.

a State two reasons why Yee opened a suspense account.

The following errors were later discovered:

1 No entry had been made for goods costing $220 taken by Yee for personal use.

2 $679 paid to Kuso, a credit supplier, had been recorded in his account as $697.

3 Motor vehicle expenses, $199, had been debited to the motor vehicles account.

4 Rent received from a tenant, $180, had been debited to the rent payable account.

5 No entry had been made in the ledger for office expenses, $15, paid from petty cash.

6 The sales returns journal was undercast by $100.

b Prepare the entries in Yee's journal to correct the above errors. Narratives are required.

c Prepare the suspense account in Yee's ledger to show the required amendments. Start with the balance arising from the difference on the trial balance.

d Explain why not all of the corrections require an entry in the suspense account. Illustrate your answer with an example from the above information.

10 A trial balance prepared for Nyasha on 30 June 20–6 did not balance. The debit side totalled $167 680 and the credit side totalled $167 934. Nyasha entered the difference in a suspense account and prepared a draft income statement which showed a profit for the year of $21 410.

The following errors were later discovered:

1 The purchases journal had been overcast by $100.

2 $285 received from J Khan had been entered in the account of K Khan, another credit customer, in the sales ledger.

3 Goods, $95, returned to a credit supplier, Begum Stores, had been correctly recorded in the purchases returns journal, but had been credited to the account of Begum Stores.

4 A cheque, $74, for electricity had been correctly recorded in the bank account, but no other entry had been made.

5 Discount allowed, $90, had been omitted from the trial balance.

a Prepare the entries in Nyasha's journal to correct the above errors. Narratives are **not** required.

b Prepare the suspense account in Nyasha's ledger to show the necessary amendments. Start with the balance arising from the difference on the trial balance.

c Using your answer to **b**, state whether you consider that all the errors in Nyasha's books have been discovered. Give a reason for your answer.

d Prepare a statement to show the corrected profit for the year ended 30 June 20–6.

11 Osama is a trader. He has only a limited knowledge of book-keeping, but attempted to prepare a set of financial statements at the end of his first financial year on 31 December 20–5. The statement of financial position he prepared is shown below.

	$
Non-current assets at cost	17 500
Inventory	1 830
Trade receivables	2 650
Drawings	5 100
	27 080
Capital at 1 January 20–5	21 000
Profit for the year	1 710
Trade payables	3 100
Bank overdraft	790
	26 600
Suspense account	480
	27 080

When the books were checked the following errors were discovered:

1 The non-current assets should have been depreciated by 10% on cost.

2 The sales account had been undercast by $500.

3 No adjustment had been made for rates and insurance, $40, paid in advance.

4 No entry had been made for goods costing $280 taken by Osama for personal use.

5 The bank statement on 31 December 20–5 showed bank charges of $81. No entry had been made in Osama's books.

6 A provision for doubtful debts of 2% of the trade receivables should have been made.

7 Office expenses, $20, have been correctly recorded in the bank account, but no other entry has been made.

a Prepare a statement to show Osama's corrected profit for the year ended 31 December 20–5.

b Prepare a corrected statement of financial position of Osama at 31 December 20–5. Use a suitable form of presentation.

TIP

This question requires the skill of analysis. You need to analyse the effects of each of the errors on the balancing of the trial balance, on the profit for the year and on the items in the statement of financial position.

12 Safiya maintains a full set of accounting records and prepares control accounts at the end of each month.

She provided the following information:

20–5		$	
July 1	Purchases ledger control account balance	1 740	credit
	Purchases ledger control account balance	20	debit
31	Totals for the month		
	Purchases journal	1 860	
	Purchases returns journal	29	
	Cheques paid to credit suppliers	1 617	
	Discounts received from credit suppliers	33	
	Interest charged by credit supplier on overdue account	15	
	Contra item transferred from the sales ledger to the purchases ledger	90	

a Prepare Safiya's purchases ledger control account for the month of July 20–5. There is only one balance on the account at the end of the month.

b State where Safiya obtained the relevant figure for **each** of the following items:

i cheques paid to credit suppliers

ii discounts received

iii contra item.

c Explain how the contra item may have arisen.

TIP
This question requires the skill of knowledge and understanding. You need to know about the principles of preparing control accounts. You need to understand how that knowledge should be applied to satisfy the requirements of the question.

13 The following information was obtained from the books of Marvan:

20–9		$	
March 1	Balance brought down on sales ledger control account	4 520	debit
Totals of journals for March 20–9 were:			
	Sales	5 180	
	Sales returns	210	
The cash book for March 20–9 showed:			
	Cheques and bank transfers received from credit customers	3 977	
	Discounts allowed to credit customers	123	
The journal entries included:			
	Irrecoverable debt written off	58	
	Inter ledger transfer	45	
	Interest charged on overdue customer's account	10	
April 1	Sales ledger credit balances	90	

a Prepare Marvan's sales ledger control account for the month ended 31 March 20–9.

b Explain **two** reasons why Marvan should prepare a sales ledger control account.

c State **two** reasons which may have resulted in a credit balance on a credit customer's account.

d Calculate the rate of cash discount Marvan allowed his credit customers.

14 Jaswant is a trader. She maintains a full set of accounting records and provided the following information for the month of February 20–8:

		$
Feb 1	Amount owing to credit suppliers	3 490
	Amount owing by credit customers	4 830
28	Goods sold on credit	5 810
	Goods purchased on credit	3 920
	Goods returned to credit suppliers	42
	Goods returned by credit customers	64
	Cheques and bank transfers received from credit customers	4 365
	Cheques and bank transfers paid to credit suppliers	2 925
	Discounts allowed	135
	Discounts received	75
	Balance in sales ledger transferred to purchases ledger	212
Mar 1	Debit balance on credit supplier's account	46
	Credit balance on credit customer's account	101

a Select the relevant figures and prepare Jaswant's purchases ledger control account for the month ended 28 February 20–8.

b The total of the credit balances in the purchases ledger on 28 February 20–8 did not agree with the credit balance on the purchases ledger control account. Explain the significance of this.

c Explain why Jaswant writes up her purchases ledger control account from the books of original entry and not from her purchases ledger.

15 Sourav maintains a full set of accounting records and prepares control accounts at the end of each month.

a State **three** advantages of preparing control accounts.

b State **three** sources of information for the items in a sales ledger control account.

Sourav provided the following information at 31 July 20–3:

		$
Jul 1	Amount owing by credit customers	19 760
	Provision for doubtful debts	990
	Credit balance on credit customer's account	344
31	Totals for month:	
	Cash sales	14 350
	Credit sales	24 145
	Cheques received from credit customers	18 870
	Cheque received (included in the above figure) later dishonoured	460
	Discount allowed	370
	Discount received	615
	Irrecoverable debts written off	175
	Returns by credit customers	738
	Sales ledger balances transferred to purchases ledger	242
Aug 1	Credit balance on credit customer's account	196

c   Select the relevant figures and prepare Sourav's sales ledger control account for the month ended 31 July 20–3.

d   Select **two** items listed above that should not be included in the sales ledger control account and explain why they do not appear.

After the preparation of the purchases ledger control account for July 20–3, it was found that the purchases returns journal had been overcast by $100.

e   Explain how this error would affect the credit balance on the purchases ledger control account on 1 August 20–3.

TIP

Parts **a–d** of this question require the skill of knowledge and understanding. You need to know the principles of preparing a sales ledger control account and you need to understand how to apply those principles to the given scenario.

Part **e** requires the skill of analysis. You need to analyse the effects of the error on the balance of the control account.

16 a Explain the meaning of **each** of the following terms:

    i margin

    ii mark-up.

b At the end of her second year of trading, Ansie provided the following information:

	$
Revenue	40 200
Purchases	31 600
Sales returns	200
Purchases returns	400
Inventory 1 August 20–8	2 300

Ansie omitted to calculate the value of her inventory on 31 July 20–9 and did not maintain any inventory records during the year. She sells all goods at a profit margin of 25%.

Calculate, by means of a trading section of an income statement, the value of Ansie's inventory on 31 July 20–9.

TIP
This question requires the skill of knowledge and understanding. You need to know the meaning of the terms margin and mark-up. You need to understand how to apply that knowledge to calculate the missing figure.

17 Some of Govinder's accounting records were badly damaged when his premises were flooded.

He was able to provide the following information:

Inventory 1 January 20–1	$3 000
Inventory 31 December 20–1	$4 000
Rate of inventory turnover	13.5 times
Mark-up	20%

Prepare a detailed trading section of the income statement for the year ended 31 December 20–1.

18 Belinda runs a secretarial agency. She does not maintain many accounting records.

On 1 September 20–5, she provided the following information:

	$
Premises at cost	80 000
Fixtures and equipment at cost	6 000
Motor vehicles at cost	11 800
Trade receivables	4 100
Wages accrued	600
Balance at bank	2 500
Long term loan – HiFinance Limited	20 000

During the year ended 31 August 20–6, Belinda paid off half of the long term loan. She purchased new equipment costing $1 000 and withdrew $4 500 from the bank for personal use.

At 31 August 20–6, the fixtures and equipment and motor vehicles should be depreciated by 20% on the cost of the assets held on that date.

On 31 August 20–6, wages accrued amounted to $570, trade receivables amounted to $4 750 and there was a bank overdraft of $1 420.

a   Prepare a statement of affairs of Belinda at 1 September 20–5 showing the total capital at that date.

b   Prepare a statement of affairs of Belinda at 31 August 20–6 showing the total capital at that date.

c   Prepare a statement to show the calculation of Belinda's profit or loss for the year ended 31 August 20–6.

d   Explain to Belinda the disadvantages of not maintaining a full set of accounting records.

19 Nabil is a trader. He has not kept a full set of accounting records, but was able to provide the following information:

	1 April 20–7 $	31 March 20–8 $
Inventory	5 300	6 050
Trade receivables	4 150	4 970
Trade payables	3 950	4 080
Machinery at cost	38 000	38 000
Equipment at cost	13 500	13 500
Motor vehicles at cost	9 400	9 400
Petty cash	100	100
Balance at bank	1 580	–
Bank overdraft	–	5 864
Other receivables	240	–
Other payables	120	170
Long term loan from El Tahrir Loans	15 000	5 000

At 31 March 20–8 Nabil decided that the machinery should be depreciated by 20% on cost and the equipment should be depreciated by 15% on cost. At that date, the motor vehicle was revalued at $8 100.

On 31 March 20–8, a debt of $170 should be written off as irrecoverable. Nabil decided to create a provision for doubtful debts of 2% of the remaining trade receivables.

a   Prepare a statement of affairs of Nabil at 1 April 20–7 showing his total capital at that date.

b   Prepare a statement of affairs of Nabil at 31 March 20–8 showing his total capital at that date.

During the year ended 31 March 20–8, Nabil introduced a further $10 000 as capital. His drawings during the same period were $4 400 in cash and goods costing $685.

c   Prepare a statement showing the calculation of the profit or loss for the year for Nabil for the year ended 31 March 20–8.

Nabil is concerned that his profits have been falling/losses have been increasing during the last few years.

d   Advise Nabil of three ways in which he could increase profits/reduce losses.

> **TIP**
>
> Parts **a–c** of this question require the skill of knowledge and understanding. You need to know the steps required to calculate profit when there are only a few accounting records and to understand how to apply that knowledge to the given scenario.
>
> Part **d** requires the skill of analysis. You need to analyse the ways in which the performance of the business can be improved.

20 Chi Chi is a trader. Her financial year ends on 31 October. She provided the following information:

	1 November 20–4 $	31 October 20–5 $
Inventory	3 870	3 100
Trade receivables	4 970	5 250
Trade payables	6 250	6 950

During the year ended 31 October 20–5:

	$
Cheques paid to credit suppliers	43 290
Cheques received from credit customers	43 120
Discounts received	1 110
Discounts allowed	880
Cash sales	15 720
Cash purchases	330

a Calculate Chi Chi's credit sales for the year ended 31 October 20–5 by means of a total trade receivables account.

b Calculate Chi Chi's credit purchases for the year ended 31 October 20–5 by means of a total trade payables account.

c Prepare the trading section of Chi Chi's income statement for the year ended 31 October 20–5.

d Calculate Chi Chi's rate of inventory turnover for the year ended 31 October 20–5.

21 Balbir started a business on 1 May 20–4. He introduced capital of $80 000. This included premises, $50 000, machinery, $14 000, and the remainder was deposited into a business bank account.

Balbir had only limited knowledge of book-keeping and he did not maintain a full set of accounting records.

All purchases and sales were made on credit terms. Cheques received from credit customers were banked on the day of receipt. Credit suppliers and all other payments were paid by cheque.

During the year ended 30 April 20–5:

Receipts	$	Payments by cheque	$
Cheques from credit customers	68 385	Credit suppliers	57 915
		Operating expenses	160
		Machinery repairs	120
		Wages	6 556
		Rates and insurance	930
		Drawings	9 850

a Prepare a summarised bank account for the year ended 30 April 20–5. Balance the account and bring down the balance on 1 May 20–5.

During the year ended 30 April 20–5 Balbir returned goods, $150, to credit suppliers. Discounts of $1 485 were received from credit suppliers. At 30 April 20–5, $17 650 was owed to credit suppliers.

b Calculate, by means of a total trade payables account, the purchases for the year ended 30 April 20–5.

Sales during the year ended 30 April 20–5 amounted to $83 000 and sales returns amounted to $970. Discounts allowed to credit customers totalled $2 115. At 30 April 20–5, a debt of $230 should be written off as irrecoverable.

c Calculate, by means of a total trade receivables account, the amount owed by credit customers on 30 April 20–5.

During the year ended 30 April 20–5, Balbir took goods costing $1 550 for his own use.

Balbir did not value his inventory on 30 April 20–5.

All goods were sold at a margin of 20%.

d Prepare a detailed trading section of Balbir's income statement for the year ended 30 April 20–5, showing the value of the inventory on 30 April 20–5.

At 30 April 20–5, it was decided that the machinery should be depreciated by 10% on cost.

e Starting with the gross profit calculated in **d**, prepare the profit and loss section of the income statement to calculate the profit for the year ended 30 April 20–5.

f Prepare Balbir's statement of affairs at 30 April 20–5.

22 The treasurer of the Zabeel Social Club provided the following information for the year ended 31 December 20–2:

		$
Subscriptions received	for the year ended 31 December 20–1	40
	for the year ended 31 December 20–2	1 800
	for the year ending 31 December 20–3	60
Clubhouse rent paid	for the year ended 31 December 20–2	780
	for the year ending 31 December 20–3	45
Insurance paid for the year ended 31 December 20–2		320
General expenses paid for the year ended 31 December 20–2		515
Cost of new furniture		1 100

On 1 January 20–2, there was a debit balance of $420 on the receipts and payments account.

a Prepare the receipts and payments account of the Zabeel Social Club for the year ended 31 December 20–2.

b State **two** differences between a receipts and payments account and an income and expenditure account.

c Explain the reason for the figure you inserted in the receipts and payments account for **each** of the following:

   i subscriptions

   ii rent.

d Explain the significance of the balance in the receipts and payments account:

   i on 1 January 20–2

   ii on 31 December 20–2.

e Explain why the depreciation of the club's non-current assets does not appear in the receipts and payments account.

TIP

This question requires the skill of knowledge and understanding. You need to know about the preparation of the financial statements of a club. You need to understand how to apply that knowledge to the particular items raised in the scenario.

23 The Mahamba Sports Club had the following assets and liabilities on 1 April 20–5:

	$
Clubhouse at cost	57 000
Sports equipment at book value	15 000
Cash at bank	3 000
Subscriptions owing by members	200
Insurance prepaid	140

The following is a summary of the receipts and payments for the year ended 31 March 20–6:

Receipts	$	Payments	$
Subscriptions	5 500	Insurance for 12 months to 30 June 20–6	624
Competition entrance fees	950	Competition expenses	370
Proceeds of sale of old sports equipment	1 000	Office expenses	183
Interest received	30	New sports equipment	2 200
		Repairs and maintenance	97

The following additional information is available:

1 The old equipment disposed of during the year was sold at book value.

2 Sports equipment is depreciated by 10% on the book value of equipment held at the end of each financial year.

3 The club has 500 members who each pay an annual subscription of $10.

a Prepare the income and expenditure account of the Mahamba Sports Club for the year ended 31 March 20–6.

b Prepare the statement of financial position of the Mahamba Sports Club at 31 March 20–6.

24 The following is the receipts and payments account of the Ansari Rugby Club for the year ended 31 May 20–6:

Receipts	$	Payments	$
Opening balance	769	Rent	2 000
Subscriptions	4 750	Rates	1 950
Proceeds of sale of old equipment	198	General expenses	486
Sales of refreshments	290	New equipment	2 000
Closing balance	918	Repairs to equipment	282
		Cost of refreshments	207
	6 925		6 925

The following additional information is available at 31 May 20–6:

1 Subscriptions prepaid amounted to $90.

2 Subscriptions accrued amounted to $170.

3 Rates prepaid amounted to $30.

4 General expenses accrued amounted to $93.

5 The equipment sold had a book value of $250.

6 Equipment is to be depreciated by $380.

a Prepare an income and expenditure account of the Ansari Rugby Club for the year ended 31 May 20–6.

b Select **one** item appearing in the receipts and payments account which should not be included in the income and expenditure account and explain why it does not appear.

c Select **one** item appearing in the income and expenditure account which is not included in the receipts and payments account and explain why it does not appear.

d In connection with a club, explain what is meant by accumulated fund and how it arises.

25 The Scar Top Athletics Society was formed on 1 October 20–4. The treasurer provided the following information at the end of the first financial year:

		$
Receipts	Subscriptions	4 820
	Shop sales	8 100
	Competition ticket sales	1 020
	Interest received	44
Payments	General expenses	585
	Purchase of shop fittings	1 000
	Payments to shop credit suppliers	3 905
	Wages of shop assistant	3 750
	Rent and rates	3 190
	Insurance	1 070
	Competition expenses	950

At 30 September 20–5:

1   Subscriptions prepaid amounted to $160.

2   $415 was owing to shop suppliers.

3   General expenses prepaid amounted to $15.

4   $284 rent was accrued.

5   The shop inventory was valued at $370.

6   Shop fittings are to be depreciated by $150.

a   Prepare the income statement of the Scar Top Athletics Society shop for the year ended 30 September 20–5.

b   Prepare the income and expenditure account of the Scar Top Athletics Society for the year ended 30 September 20–5.

The club committee is not very happy about the first year's results. A member of the committee has suggested that increasing the annual subscription by 10% would increase the bank balance.

c   Advise the committee on whether or not to go ahead with this proposal.

TIP

Parts **a–b** of this question requires the skill of knowledge and understanding. You need to know the principles of preparing financial statements of a club and understand how to apply those principles to the information provided.

Part **c** requires the skill of evaluation. You need to evaluate the advantages and disadvantages of the proposal and draw a reasoned conclusion.

26   The treasurer of the Kaunda Street Music Society did not maintain a full set of accounting records but was able to provide the following information:

	1 December 20–1 $	30 November 20–2 $
Subscriptions owing by members	330	420
Subscriptions prepaid by members	–	150
Inventory of refreshments	466	514
Trade payables for refreshments	319	293

During the year ended 30 November 20–2:

	$
Subscriptions received	4 860
Payments to credit suppliers for refreshments	3 861
Receipts from sale of refreshments	5 982

The subscriptions received included $300 of the amount accrued on 1 December 20–1. The subscriptions still outstanding for the year ended 30 November 20–1 should be written off as irrecoverable.

a Prepare the subscriptions account for the year ended 30 November 20–2.

b Calculate the credit purchases for the year ended 30 November 20–2.

c Prepare the refreshments income statement of the Kaunda Street Music Society for the year ended 30 November 20–2.

27 The financial year of the Island Drama Society ends on 31 July.

The treasurer has not maintained a full set of accounting records but was able to provide the following information:

At 1 August 20–3:

	$
Premises at cost	33 000
Equipment at book value	17 500
Subscriptions prepaid by members	150
Subscriptions owed by members	320
Cash at bank	2 890
Staff wages accrued	350
Insurance prepaid	120

During the year ended 31 July 20–4:

Receipts	$	Payments	$
Subscriptions	5 880	Insurance for 12 months	
Concert ticket sales	1 943	to 30 September 20–4	744
Sale of old equipment (at book value)	500	Concert expenses	1 007
		Wages	2 290
		New equipment	2 900

General expenses were paid during the year, but no record was made of the amount spent.

At 31 July 20–4:

1 There was $3 402 in the bank account.

2 Wages accrued amounted to $290.

3 Equipment is being depreciated by 20% per annum on the book value of equipment held at the end of each financial year.

4 Subscriptions owed by members amounted to $90.

a Calculate the Island Drama Society's accumulated fund on 1 August 20–3.

b Calculate the amount paid for general expenses during the year ended 31 July 20–4.

c Prepare the Island Drama Society's income and expenditure account for the year ended 31 July 20–4.

d Prepare the Island Drama Society's statement of financial position at 31 July 20–4.

28 Jayron is a trader. He would like to expand his business and is considering forming a partnership with his friend Abubker.

   a Advise Jayron of the advantages and disadvantages of remaining as a sole trader.

   b Advise Jayron of the advantages and disadvantages of trading in partnership.

   c Explain to Jayron why it is necessary for a partnership to prepare an appropriation account as part of the annual financial statements.

   d Explain to Jayron the difference between a capital account and a current account and why both a capital and a current account should be maintained for each partner.

29 Precious and Marcia are in partnership. Their partnership agreement includes the following:

Interest on capital to be paid at 5% per annum.

Interest on drawings to be charged at 3%.

Marcia to receive an annual salary of $12 000.

Profits and losses to be shared 3:2.

On 1 June 20–1 the balances on the partners' capital accounts were:

	$
Precious	90 000
Marcia	70 000

During the year ended 31 May 20–2 the partners' drawings were:

	$
Precious	15 000
Marcia	21 000

The profit for the year ended 31 May 20–2 was $25 100.

   a Prepare the profit and loss appropriation account of Precious and Marcia for the year ended 31 May 20–2.

   b State why it is advisable for partners to draw up a partnership agreement when they form a partnership.

   c State why a partnership agreement may provide for **each** of the following:

   i interest on capital

   ii interest on drawings

   iii partnership salaries.

TIP

This question requires the skill of knowledge and understanding. You need to know the principles of preparing a partnership appropriation account and the contents of a partnership agreement. You need to understand how to apply that knowledge to the business described.

30 John and David are in partnership sharing profits and losses equally.

The following information is available for the year ended 31 January 20–8:

		$
Profit for the year		14 200
Interest on drawings	John	220
	David	180
Interest on capital	John	1 500
	David	1 200
Partners' salaries	John	8 000
	David	6 000

a Calculate the profit/loss available for distribution. Show how this is divided between the partners.

On 1 February 20–7, the balances on the partners' current accounts were as follows:

	$	
John	1 750	debit
David	2 260	credit

During the year ended 31 January 20–8, the partners' drawings were as follows:

	$
John	11 000
David	8 000

b Write up the current accounts of John and David for the year ended 31 January 20–8 as they would appear in the ledger of the partnership. Balance the accounts on 31 January 20–8 and bring down the balances on 1 February 20–8.

On 1 February 20–8 the balances on the partners' capital accounts were as follows:

	$
John	50 000
David	40 000

On 2 February 20–8, John transferred $3 000 from the debit balance on his current account to his capital account. On 3 February, David paid additional capital into the business bank account so that his capital was equal to that of John.

c Write up the capital accounts of John and David for the month of February 20–8 as they would appear in the ledger of the partnership. Balance the accounts and bring down the balances on 1 March 20–8.

31 Terry and Candy are in partnership. Their financial year ends on 31 August.

Their partnership agreement included the following:

Interest on capital to be allowed at 6% per annum.

Interest on drawings to be charged at 4%.

Candy to receive an annual salary of $17 000.

Profits and losses to be shared 2:1.

The balances on the partners' accounts on 1 September 20–4 were as follows:

		$	
Capital accounts	Terry	80 000	
	Candy	50 000	
Current accounts	Terry	3 250	debit
	Candy	1 050	credit

During the year ended 31 August 20–5, the partners' drawings were as follows:

	$
Terry	12 000
Candy	18 000

The income statement for the year ended 31 August 20–5 showed a profit for the year of $39 500.

a Prepare the profit and loss appropriation account of Terry and Candy for the year ended 31 August 20–5.

b Write up the current accounts of Terry and Candy for the year ended 31 August 20–5 as they would appear in the ledger of the partnership. Balance the accounts on 31 August 20–5 and bring down the balances on 1 September 20–5.

c Prepare a relevant extract from the statement of financial position of Terry and Candy at 31 August 20–5 to show their capital and current accounts.

32 Bill and Ben are in partnership. Their financial year ends on 31 March. They share profits and losses in proportion to the capital invested.

On 1 April 20–3, the balances on the partners' capital and current accounts were:

	Capital account	Current account
	$	$
Bill	50 000	2 950 credit
Ben	25 000	1 700 debit

During the year ended 31 March 20–4, the partners' drawings were:

	$
Bill	6 000
Ben	12 000

The following information was extracted from the profit and loss appropriation account for the year ended 31 March 20–4:

	$	$
Profit for the year		15 150
Interest on drawings – Bill	180	
Ben	360	540
		15 690
Interest on capital – Bill	1 500	
Ben	750	
	2 250	
Salary – Ben	6 000	8 250
Profit available for distribution		7 440

At 31 March 20–4 the following information was available:

	$
Non-current assets at book value	87 100
Current assets	38 300
Current liabilities	40 000
Non-current liabilities	12 000

a Prepare the statement of financial position of Bill and Ben at 31 March 20–4. The capital and current account of each partner should be shown. The calculation of the current account balances may either be shown within the statement or as separate ledger accounts.

b Explain why Bill is concerned about the change in the balance of Ben's current account during the year.

33 Ravi and Iqra own a garden maintenance business. Their financial year ends on 30 April.

The partnership agreement provides for:

loan interest at 6% per annum on loans from partners

interest on capital at 5% per annum

profits and losses to be shared equally.

The trial balance of Ravi and Iqra at 30 April 20–3 was as follows:

	$	$
Capital account Ravi 1 May 20–2		70 000
Capital account Iqra 1 May 20–2		40 000
Current account Ravi 1 May 20–2		1 020
Current account Iqra 1 May 20–2	150	
Drawings Ravi	12 200	
Drawings Iqra	11 820	
Loan – Ravi		20 000
Loan interest	600	
Premises at cost	70 000	
Equipment at cost	21 000	
Provision for depreciation of equipment		4 200
Motor vehicles at cost	32 000	
Provision for depreciation of motor vehicles		8 000
Fees		106 075
Wages	57 870	
Repairs to equipment	2 720	
Motor vehicle expenses	3 030	
Insurance	3 450	
Operating expenses	2 765	
Printing and stationery	320	
Irrecoverable debts	220	
Provision for doubtful debts		360
Trade receivables	8 000	
Bank	23 280	
Cash	2 540	
Trade payables		2 310
	251 965	251 965

The following additional information is available:

1 At 30 April 20–3, wages, $1 090, were accrued.

2 At 30 April 20–3, insurance, $360, was prepaid.

3 Equipment is being depreciated at 20% per annum using the straight line method.

4 Motor vehicles are being depreciated at 25% per annum using the reducing balance method.

5 The provision for doubtful debts is maintained at 5% of the trade receivables at the end of each financial year.

a Prepare the income statement of Ravi and Iqra for the year ended 30 April 20–3.

b Prepare the profit and loss appropriation account of Ravi and Iqra for the year ended 30 April 20–3.

c Prepare the statement of financial position of Ravi and Iqra at 30 April 20–3.

34 Nicola and Lydia are traders. Their financial year ends on 31 October. The following trial balance was drawn up on 31 October 20–8 after the calculation of the gross profit:

	$	$
Capital account Nicola 1 November 20–7		10 000
Capital account Lydia 1 November 20–7		10 000
Current account Nicola 1 November 20–7		118
Current account Lydia 1 November 20–7		236
Drawings Nicola	2 100	
Drawings Lydia	1 900	
Discount received		630
Discount allowed	940	
Wages	5 670	
Rent and rates	2 120	
Furniture and fittings at cost	10 500	
Provision for depreciation of furniture and fittings		2 100
Motor vehicles at cost	19 000	
Provision for depreciation of motor vehicles		6 840
Motor vehicle expenses	950	
Trade payables		3 459
Trade receivables	3 850	
Provision for doubtful debts		179
Irrecoverable debts	540	
Bank		1 029
Petty cash	50	
5% loan (repayable 1 January 20–9)		4 000
Loan interest	200	
Commission receivable		1 090
Office expenses	3 116	
Inventory 31 October 20–8	7 745	
Gross profit		19 000
	58 681	58 681

The following additional information is available:

1 At 31 October 20–8, motor vehicle expenses, $105, were outstanding and rates, $48, were prepaid.

2 The furniture and fittings are being depreciated at 10% per annum using the straight line method.

3 The motor vehicles are being depreciated at 20% per annum using the reducing balance method.

4 The provision for doubtful debts is maintained at 4% of the trade receivables at the end of each financial year.

5 The partnership agreement provides for interest on capital at 4% per annum and for profits and losses to be shared Nicola $\frac{3}{5}$ and Lydia $\frac{2}{5}$.

121

a Prepare the income statement of Nicola and Lydia for the year ended 31 October 20–8. Start with the gross profit.

b Prepare the profit and loss appropriation account of Nicola and Lydia for the year ended 31 October 20–8.

c Prepare the statement of financial position of Nicola and Lydia at 31 October 20–8.

35 Yassin and Muneen are in partnership, sharing profits and losses in the ratio 2:1.

Their financial year ends on 30 November.

Despite having little accounting knowledge, Yassin decided to attempt a set of financial statements for the year ended 30 November 20–6. The statement of financial position he prepared was as follows:

	$
Premises at cost	50 000
Machinery at cost	24 000
Furniture and equipment at cost	18 000
Inventory	23 200
Trade receivables	11 600
Bank overdraft	5 150
Drawings – Yassin	8 400
Muneen	6 600
	146 950
Trade payables	13 520
Provision for depreciation of machinery	4 800
Provision for depreciation of furniture and equipment	3 600
Capital – Yassin	55 000
Muneen	40 000
Profit for the year	19 780
	136 700
Balance	10 250
	146 950

The following errors were then discovered:

1 No entry had been made for depreciation of furniture and equipment for the year. This asset should be depreciated by 10% per annum using the straight line method.

2 A provision for doubtful debts of $232 should have been created at 30 November 20–6.

3 No adjustment had been made for insurance, $60, prepaid at 30 November 20–6.

4 The inventory at 30 November 2006 included goods costing $1 200 which were damaged and regarded as unsaleable.

5 Petty cash, $50, had been omitted from the statement of financial position.

a Calculate the corrected profit for the year ended 30 November 20–6. Show the division of the profit between the partners.

b Prepare the corrected statement of financial position of Yassin and Muneen at 30 November 20–6, using a suitable form of presentation.

36 The Apollo Manufacturing Company provided the following information for the year ended 30 June 20–5:

	$
Inventory of raw material 1 July 20–4	23 500
Inventory of raw material 30 June 20–5	21 500
Work in progress 1 July 20–4	9 880
Work in progress 30 June 20–5	10 040
For the year ended 30 June 20–5:	
Purchases of raw material	287 560
Direct factory wages	199 450
Direct expenses	8 740
Indirect factory expenses	186 330

a Explain **each** of the following terms:

  i work in progress

  ii direct expenses

  iii indirect factory expenses.

b Calculate the prime cost.

c Calculate the cost of production.

37 a Explain the purpose of a manufacturing account.

  b Explain the difference between the following:

    i prime cost and cost of production

    ii direct labour and indirect labour.

c The Vasant Vihar Manufacturing Company provided the following information:

	1 January 20–4 $	31 December 20–4 $
Inventory – Raw material	16 650	17 720
Work in progress	18 222	19 115
Factory operatives' wages outstanding	1 850	1 990
Factory insurance prepaid	760	800

For the year ended 31 December 20–4:

	$
Purchases of raw material	210 500
Carriage on raw materials	3 120
Wages – Factory operatives	197 280
Factory supervisors	32 100
Factory rent and rates	15 500
Factory insurance	4 800
Factory general expenses	12 700

The factory machinery cost $56 000. The depreciation on factory machinery up to 31 December 20–3 totalled $20 160. The machinery is being depreciated using the reducing balance method at the rate of 20% per annum.

Prepare the manufacturing account of The Vasant Vihar Manufacturing Company for the year ended 31 December 20–4.

38 Homi Modi Manufacturers provided the following information for the year ended 31 March 20–9:

At 1 April 20–8:	$
Inventory of finished goods	16 380
Inventory of raw material	7 850
Work in progress	6 120
For the year ended 31 March 20–9:	
Revenue	400 500
Purchases of finished goods	22 540
Purchases of raw material	98 730
Carriage on raw material	2 030
Wages – Factory direct	95 680
Factory indirect	37 250
Office	74 600
Sales people	44 870
Insurance	10 500
Light and heat	13 300
Operating expenses	18 210
Depreciation – Factory machinery	9 750
Office equipment	3 150

At 31 March 20–9: $

	$
Inventory of finished goods	13 280
Inventory of raw material	8 170
Work in progress	7 470

The expenses are apportioned as follows:

Insurance and operating expenses – Factory $\frac{2}{3}$ and office $\frac{1}{3}$

Light and heat – Factory $\frac{4}{5}$ and office $\frac{1}{5}$

Select the relevant figures and prepare:

a the manufacturing account of Homi Modi Manufacturers for the year ended 31 March 20–9

b the trading section of the income statement of Homi Modi Manufacturers for the year ended 31 March 20–9.

The managers of Homi Modi Manufacturers are concerned that the gross profit has decreased over the last four years.

c Advise the managers on ways in which the gross profit could be increased.

TIP

Parts **a** and **b** of this question require the skill of knowledge and understanding as you need to know how to prepare a manufacturing account and an income statement of a manufacturing business and understand how to apply that knowledge to the given scenario.

Part **c** of the question requires the skill of analysis. You need to analyse the ways in which the gross profit could be increased.

39 Strand Road Manufacturing Limited makes cooking sauces. Their financial year ends on 30 June. The following information is available:

	1 July 20–4 $	30 June 20–5 $
Inventory of raw material	2 160	2 870
Inventory of jars and labels	3 120	3 390
Inventory of finished goods	8 190	7 940
Work in progress	1 195	1 825

	$
For the year ended 30 June 20–5:	
Revenue	295 600
Purchases of raw material	26 830
Purchases of jars and labels	15 250
Carriage on raw material	1 980
Direct factory wages	32 560
Indirect factory wages	6 120
Factory light and power	9 440
Factory operating expenses	4 910
Depreciation – Factory machinery	5 500

a Prepare the manufacturing account of Strand Road Manufacturing Limited for the year ended 30 June 20–5.

b Prepare the trading section of the income statement of Strand Road Manufacturing Limited for the year ended 30 June 20–5.

40 Anais and Emi are considering converting their partnership business into a limited company. They require some advice about limited companies.

a Explain the meaning of the term 'limited liability'.

b Advise the partners of the advantages and disadvantages of operating as a limited company.

c Explain the meaning of the following terms used in connection with limited companies:

i issued share capital

ii called-up share capital

iii paid-up share capital

d Explain the meaning of the term 'equity' in connection with limited companies.

41 The statement of financial position LMS Limited showed that the capital structure consisted of ordinary shares, preference shares, general reserve and retained earnings.

a Explain the difference between ordinary shares and preference shares.

b State why it is important to understand the difference between redeemable preference shares and non-redeemable preference shares.

c State how the general reserve has arisen.

d State what is meant by the term 'retained earnings'.

The directors of LMS Limited want to expand the company and need to raise additional funds.

They are considering making an issue of 5% debentures.

e Explain the difference between debentures and ordinary shares.

42 DW Limited provided the following information at 31 May 20–8:

	$
Issued share capital ordinary shares of $0.5 each	350 000
6% redeemable preference shares of $1 each	150 000
General reserve	32 000
Retained earnings	8 900
5% debentures	50 000

a Calculate the number of ordinary shares DW Limited has issued.

b Calculate the total annual dividend (in $) payable on the preference shares.

c Calculate the total amount of interest (in $) payable on the debentures.

d Explain why the retained earnings have arisen.

e Explain how the general reserve has arisen.

f Explain the difference between dividends proposed and dividends paid.

g Explain why debenture interest paid appears in the income statement of a limited company but ordinary share dividends paid appear in the statement of changes in equity.

TIP
This question requires the skill of knowledge and understanding. You need to know the different ways in which a company raises long term funds and understand how to apply that knowledge to the calculations and explanations required by the question.

43 The financial year of LY Limited ends on 31 July. The following information is available for the year ended 31 July 20–3:

Issued share capital	$
Ordinary shares of $1 each	80 000
5% redeemable preference shares of $1 each	50 000

The profit for the year ended 31 July 20–3 **before** preference share dividend was $20 000.

The retained earnings on 1 August 20–2 amounted to $7 500.

During the year ended 31 July 20–3:

1 An interim dividend of $2\frac{1}{2}$% was paid on the redeemable preference shares.

2 An interim dividend of 2% was paid on the ordinary shares.

At 31 July 20–3:

1 Six months' redeemable preference share dividend was to be accrued.

2 It was decided to transfer $8 000 to general reserve.

3 It was decided that an ordinary share dividend of 7% would be paid.

a Calculate the profit for the year ended 31 July 20–3 after the dividend on the redeemable preference shares.

b Prepare the statement of changes in equity of LY Limited for the year ended 31 July 20–3.

44 H Limited provided the following information:

	$
Issued share capital:	
6% redeemable preference shares of $1 each	100 000
5% redeemable preference shares of $1 each	60 000
Ordinary shares of $0.50 each	200 000
General reserve	21 000
4% debentures	30 000

The retained earnings on 1 July 20–3 amounted to $18 500.

During the year ended 30 June 20–4, an interim dividend of $0.01 per share was paid on the ordinary shares.

The profit for the year ended 30 June 20–4 was $41 000 **before** charging debenture interest dividend on redeemable preference shares.

On 30 June 20–4:

1 A full year's debenture interest was accrued.

2 A full year's dividend on the redeemable preference shares was accrued.

3 It was decided to transfer $9 000 to general reserve.

4 It was decided to pay an ordinary share dividend of $0.02 per share.

a Calculate the profit for the year after charging debenture interest and dividend on the redeemable preference shares.

b Prepare the statement of changes in equity of H Limited for the year ended 30 June 20–4.

c Prepare a relevant extract from the statement of financial position of H Limited at 30 June 20–4 to show the equity and reserves.

45 The following balances remained on the books of KT Limited after the preparation of the income statement for the year ended 30 June 20–6:

	$
Non-current assets at cost	237 000
Provision for depreciation of non-current assets	65 000
Ordinary shares of $1 each	150 000
6% debentures	30 000
Trade receivables	38 000
Trade payables	43 000
Other receivables	4 210
Other payables	3 660
Provision for doubtful debts	950
Balance at bank	11 130
Inventory	42 000
General reserve	15 000
Interim ordinary share dividend	3 000
Retained earnings 1 July 20–5	9 620
Profit for the year ended 30 June 20–6	18 110

On 30 June 20–6 it was decided:

1   to transfer $5 000 to the general reserve

2   to pay a final ordinary share dividend of $7\frac{1}{2}$ %.

a   Prepare the statement of changes in equity of KT Limited for the year ended 30 June 20–6.

b   Prepare the statement of financial position of KT Limited at 30 June 20–6.

46 The financial year of HC Limited ends on 31 August. The following information is available:

$

Issued share capital:

Redeemable preference shares of $1 each   60 000

Ordinary shares of $1 each   100 000

The retained earnings at 1 September 20–2 were $12 500.

The profit for the year ended 31 August 20–3 was $18 200 **before** charging the dividend on redeemable preference shares.

During the year ended 31 August 20–3, an interim dividend of $3 000 was paid on the ordinary shares.

At 31 August 20–3:

1   The preference share dividend, $3 600, was accrued.

2   It was decided to transfer $5 000 to general reserve.

3   It was decided to pay a final ordinary share dividend of $6 000.

a   Calculate the profit for the year ended 31 August 20–3 after the dividend on the redeemable preference shares.

b   Calculate the retained earnings at 31 August 20–3.

c   Calculate the percentage rate of the preference share dividend for the year.

d   State the percentage rate of preference share dividend which should be paid (provided the cash is available) for the year ending 31 August 20–4.

e   Explain why it is not possible to state the percentage rate of ordinary share dividend which will be paid (provided the cash is available) for the year ending 31 August 20–4.

f   Suggest **one** reason why it was decided to make a transfer to general reserve.

g   Explain the term 'interim' in connection with the ordinary share dividend.

47 The financial year of NN Limited ends on 31 May.

After the preparation of the income statement for the year ended 31 May 20–9, the following balances remained on the books:

	$	$
Ordinary shares of $1		170 000
4% debentures		50 000
General reserve		10 000
Retained earnings 1 June 20–8		5 200
Inventory 31 May 20–9	25 320	
Trade receivables	21 400	
Trade payables		15 775
Provision for doubtful debts		428
Other receivables	833	
Other payables (debenture interest accrued)		2 000
Bank	31 300	
Premises at cost	129 000	
Machinery and equipment at cost	82 000	
Motor vehicles	28 000	
Provision for depreciation of machinery and equipment		32 800
Provision for depreciation of motor vehicles		15 750
Interim dividend on ordinary shares	3 600	
Profit for year		19 500
	321 453	321 453

At 31 May 20–9 it was decided to:

• transfer $4 000 to general reserve

• pay a final ordinary share dividend of 5%.

a Prepare the statement of changes in equity of NN Limited for the year ended 31 May 20–9.

b Prepare the statement of financial position of NN Limited at 31 May 20–9.

The directors of NN Limited wish to raise $70 000 to finance a programme of expansion. They are considering issuing additional 4% debentures.

c Discuss how the ordinary shareholders may be affected if NN Limited raised the additional funds by the issue of debentures.

TIP

Parts **a** and **b** of this question require the skill of knowledge and understanding as you need to know how to prepare the financial statements of a limited company and understand how to apply that knowledge to the given scenario.

Part **c** of the question requires the skill of analysis. You need to analyse the ways in which the ordinary shareholders may be affected by the proposal.

48 Balbir is a trader. He provided the following information:

At 1 March 20–4:		$
	Inventory	9 800

For the year ended 28 February 20–5:		
	Revenue	250 000
	Purchases	190 300
	Expenses	27 500

At 28 February 20–5:		
	Inventory	10 100
	Total current assets	33 200
	Total current liabilities	19 200
	Total non-current assets	202 000

Calculate the following ratios to two decimal places:

a gross margin

b profit margin

c rate of inventory turnover

d current ratio

e liquid (acid test) ratio

f return on capital employed (ROCE).

49 a Explain the meaning of **each** of the following terms:

   i capital owned

   ii capital employed.

  b Usha is a trader. She provided the following information:

	$
For the year ended 30 June 20–5:	
Cost of sales	120 900
Operating expenses	14 100
Gross profit	35 100
Drawings	16 000
At 30 June 20–5:	
Inventory	9 350

On 1 July 20–4 the inventory was $11 650 and Usha's capital was $150 000.

Calculate the following ratios (to two decimal places):

   i gross margin

   ii profit margin

   iii profit for the year as a percentage of Usha's capital on 30 June 20–5

   iv rate of inventory turnover.

c i State the meaning of the term working capital.

  ii State **two** disadvantages of a shortage of working capital.

  iii State **two** ways in which the working capital of a business could be improved.

  iv State how **each** of the following transactions affect the working capital. Give a reason for your answer in each case.

    1   Purchase of goods, $500, on credit.

    2   Purchase of non-current assets, $2 500, by cheque.

    3   Payment by cheque, $75, in full settlement of $80 owed to a credit supplier.

    4   Sale of goods, $1 000, on credit. The goods originally cost $800.

TIP

Parts **a, b** and **c i–iii** of this question require the skill of knowledge and understanding as you need to know the meaning of certain terms and the formulae for calculating certain ratios. You need to understand how to apply that knowledge to the requirements of the question.

Part **c iv** of the question requires the skill of analysis. You need to analyse the effect of the transactions on the working capital.

50 Ellis is a trader. He wishes to compare his position with that at the end of the previous financial year. He provided the following information:

For the year ended 31 August 20–7, his revenue amounted to $620 000, of which 75% were credit sales and 25% cash sales. His purchases were $450 000, of which 20% were cash purchases.

	$
At 31 August 20–7:	
Inventory	52 500
Trade receivables	38 000
Trade payables	41 400
Bank overdraft	5 200

a Calculate the following ratios. Calculations should be to two decimal places for **i** and **ii** and rounded up to the next whole day for **iii** and **iv**.

  i current ratio

  ii liquid (acid test) ratio

  iii trade receivables turnover

  iv trade payables turnover.

The following ratios were calculated on 31 August 20–6:

Current ratio	2.00:1
Liquid (acid test) ratio	1.60:1
Trade receivables turnover	24 days
Trade payables turnover	36 days

b Compare the ratios calculated in **a** with the above ratios.

At present, Ellis allows his credit customers a cash discount of 2% for payment within 21 days. He is thinking about discontinuing this discount.

c Advise Ellis, whether or not he should change his policy on cash discount. Give reasons for your answer.

> **TIP**
>
> Part **a** of this question requires the skill of knowledge and understanding as you need to know the formulae for calculating certain ratios. You need to understand how to apply that knowledge to the information provided in the question.
>
> Part **b** of this question requires the skill of analysis. You need to analyse the effect of the changes in the ratios.
>
> Part **c** of this question requires the skill of evaluation. You need to evaluate the advantages and disadvantages of the proposal and draw a reasoned conclusion.

51 DEC Ltd provided the following information:

	31 May 20–4 $	31 May 20–5 $
Inventory	16 700	13 300
Trade receivables		26 500
Trade payables		15 400
For the financial year ended 31 May 20–5:		
Revenue – Cash sales		105 000
Credit sales		225 000
Purchases – Credit		180 000

Credit customers were allowed a period of 30 days credit.

Credit suppliers allowed a period of 21 days credit.

a **i** Calculate the rate of inventory turnover correct to two decimal places.

   ii State **two** ways in which the rate of inventory turnover could be improved.

b **i** Calculate the trade receivables turnover rounded up to the next whole day.

   ii State whether DEC Ltd would be satisfied with the trade receivables turnover. Give a reason for your answer.

   iii State **two** ways in which the trade receivables turnover could be improved.

c **i** Calculate the trade payables turnover rounded up to the next whole day.

   ii State **one** advantage of paying the credit suppliers after the period of credit allowed.

   iii State **one** disadvantage of paying the credit suppliers after the period of credit allowed.

   iv Explain how the trade receivables turnover may affect the trade payables turnover.

52 Emma is a trader. Her financial year ends on 31 August. She provided the following information on 31 August 20–1:

	$
At 1 September 20–0:	
Capital	180 000
Ten year loan	20 000
For the year ended 31 August 20–1:	
Gross profit	42 000
Cost of sales	210 000
Expenses	12 000

a i Calculate the gross margin. The calculation should be correct to two decimal places.

   ii State **two** reasons why this ratio is important to Emma.

b i Calculate the profit margin. The calculation should be correct to two decimal places.

   ii State **two** reasons why this ratio is important to Emma.

c Explain why the difference between the gross margin and the profit margin is an important indicator of how efficiently the business is being managed.

d i Calculate the return on capital employed (ROCE). Use the total capital employed on 1 September 20–0. The calculation should be correct to two decimal places.

   ii State **two** reasons why this ratio is important to Emma.

e i Using the average inventory of $12 500, calculate the rate of inventory turnover for the year ended 31 August 20–0. The calculation should be correct to two decimal places.

   ii State **two** ways in which Emma could improve the rate of inventory turnover.

53 Anisha is a trader. Her financial year ends on 31 December. She provided the following information for the year ended 31 December 20-8:

	$
Revenue	250 000
Cost of sales	180 000
Inventory at 1 January 20–8	8 500
Inventory at 31 December 20–8	10 500
Expenses	56 000
Equity at 1 January 20–8	200 000
Drawings for the year	12 000

Anisha discovered that the following errors had been made when the financial statements for the year ended 31 December 20-8 were prepared:

1 Sales returns, $4 000, had been omitted

2 Inventory at 31 December 20-8 had been overvalued by $1 500.

Explain the effects of these errors on each of the following:

a gross profit

b rate of inventory turnover

c revenue

d expenses

e profit for the year

f equity at 31 December 20–8.

54 In addition to the owner(s) of a business, various other people are interested in the accounting statements.

    a Explain why **each** of the following would be interested in the accounts of Sandra, who owns a general store:

        i bank manager

        ii credit supplier

        iii employee

        iv potential buyer of the business.

When studying the accounting statements and using them for comparison purposes, it is important to remember that these statements do not provide a complete picture of the business.

    b Explain how **each** of the following may be regarded as a limitation of accounting statements:

        i money measurement

        ii accounting policies

        iii historic cost.

55 Dave rented premises and started a business as a clothing wholesaler on 1 June 20–3. He sells on credit to large retail stores. Dave works full time in the business. He provided the following summarised financial statements:

Income statement for the year ended 31 May 20–5		
	$	$
Revenue		230 000
Cost of sales		
Opening inventory	16 500	
Purchases	175 100	
	191 600	
Less Closing inventory	14 500	177 100
Gross profit		52 900
Expenses		34 150
Profit for the year		18 750

Statement of financial position at 31 May 20–5	
	$
Non-current assets	195 000
Current assets	28 500
	223 500
Capital	160 000
Non-current liabilities (Interest-free loan)	50 000
Current liabilities	13 500
	223 500

a Calculate the following ratios correct to two decimal places:

i gross margin

ii profit margin

iii rate of inventory turnover

iv return on capital employed

v return on capital owned (use the capital owned at 31 May 20–5)

vi current ratio

vii liquid (acid test) ratio.

Dave's sisters, Ann and Susan, own a food retailing business. All goods are sold for cash.

The business was started ten years ago. Ann and Susan now own four shop premises. They do not work in the business any more but have appointed a manager for each of their four shops.

They provided the following information on 31 May 20–5:

Gross margin	16.25%
Profit margin	14.75%
Rate of inventory turnover	24.30 times
Return on capital employed	15.20%
Return on capital owned	12.95%
Current ratio	3.25:1
Liquid (acid test) ratio	2.10:1

b Compare the ratios calculated in **a** with those given above. Suggest reasons for the differences between the ratios.

c **Excluding** any factors mentioned above in connection with Dave, Ann and Susan, explain **five** problems of inter-firm comparison.

Acknowledgements

Thanks to the following for permission to reproduce images:

Cover image: Sudarshan v/Getty Images